Behavioral Economics and Decision Making:
51 Reproducible Exercises

Dr. Richard Brynteson
Dr. Steve Manderscheid

HRD Press, Inc. • Amherst • Massachusetts

Published by: HRD Press, Inc.
22 Amherst Road
Amherst, Massachusetts 01002
1-800-822-2801 (U.S. and Canada)
413-253-3488
413-253-3490 (fax)
www.hrdpress.com

ISBN 978-1-61014-379-0

Production services by Jean Miller
Editorial services by Sally Farnham
Cover design by Eileen Klockars

Behavioral Economics and Decision Making: 51 Reproducible Exercises

Table of Contents

Preface v

    Purpose vi

About the Authors vii

Unit 1: Decision-Making Basics

1. System 1/System 2 Basics 3
2. Decision Maker's Dilemma 5
3. Choices and Criteria 7
4. Five Decision-Making Modes 9
5. The Great Paradox of Decision Making 11
6. Values and Decisions 13
7. Concerns to Clear Objectives 15
8. Working with Polarity 17
9. Decision-Making Styles 19
10. Event, Pattern, and Structure 21

Unit 2: Behavioral Economics Principles

11. Default Settings 25
12. Loss Aversion 27
13. Expert Intuition 29
14. What drives you? 31
15. Monkeys and Empathy 33
16. The Elephant, the Rider, and the Path 35
17. Anchoring and Adjustment 37
18. Lowering Cognitive Effort 39
19. Imposed Self-Control 41
20. The Law of Unintended Consequences 43
21. Value Attribution 45
22. Black Pearls 47
23. You call this work? 51
24. Nice Words, Mean Words 53
25. Availability to the Imagination 55
26. Lost in a Big Box World 61
27. Which story are you going to tell? 63
28. What is your Black Swan? 65

Unit 3: Group Decision Making

29. Five Fingers to Consensus 69
30. Divergent AND Convergent...Best of Both Worlds 71
31. The Robbery—The Power of Consensus 73
32. Concept Fan 77
33. Implications Exploration 79
34. Planning Fallacy 81

Unit 4: Dysfunctional Decision Making

35. The Abilene Paradox 85
36. The Illusion of Invulnerability 87
37. Decision Fatigue 89
38. Halos and Horns 91
39. The Memory Game 93
40. Illusion of Causality 95
41. The Wrong Tools 99
42. Throwing Away Tools 101
43. Sunk Costs 103
44. Stuck with Locked Horns 105
45. Stuck at the End of Your Nose 107
46. Wooden Headedness 109
47. Perfect, or Good Enough 111
48. Irrational Thinking 113
49. Expect Error 115
50. Structure Complex Choices 117
51. We Have Always Done It This Way 119

Bibliography 123

Preface

Why decision making with a focus on behavior economics?

First, what is *decision making*? Decision making is the mental process of selecting a best choice from among available options. When making decisions, a person makes a decision from their "gut" (past experience) and/or they use a mental or physical process to explore the implications of each perceived option. The former is called intuitive decision making, and the latter is called a rational approach. Intuitive decision making is typically viewed as deciding with little to no data collection. On the other hand, a rational decision approach typically involves collecting data, weighing alternatives, and making a decision based on an option(s) that is perceived to yield the most favorable short-term or long-term result.

Decision making is a largely unconscious process. We are usually unaware of our decision process and outcomes until they result in negative unintended consequences or they present significant rewards. We make tens of thousands of decisions every day, and each of those decisions has a consequence. Our daily decisions span from which sport coat to wear in the morning to which people we should hire and fire in the afternoon. Some decisions are important with long-term consequences, and others are insignificant. Understanding the dynamics and dysfunctions of decision making is essential for making life better.

One hallmark of a successful and effective person is his or her ability to make good decisions. It is important for people to make better decisions and avoid the stress and frustration of addressing subsequent issues related to ineffective choices. The quality of our decision making relates to the quality of our personal and work life. All success and failure can be mapped to key decisions. We do not want to have to think about our decisions; we just want to embed good decision practices that operate automatically. This comes from learning and subsequent practice. One needs to be aware of their decision processes before they can change them. Once new patterns of thinking (deciding) are integrated into practice, people can then begin to make decisions without having to stop, think, and then apply.

The way we make decisions should be of prime importance to leaders in our organizations. Leaders are required to make critical decisions in unpredictable environments every day. They often do not have the luxury of securing all the necessary information before deciding. To keep pace, they need to use their collective intelligence (intuition), key stakeholders, and concepts such as these presented in this book to guide their organizations into the future.

The exercises in this book are unique in that many are focused on behavioral economics, which is the study of the cognitive, emotional, and social forces that influence decision making. Many of the exercises explore the human psyche of decision making: essentially, what drives people to make the choices they make? People are prone to making poor decisions. They make decision errors every day—decision errors that jeopardize their well-being and the well-being of those around them. Our assumption in developing these exercises is that awareness and understanding will lead to better decision-making practice, i.e., individual, team, organization, and societal change.

Behavioral economics has its roots in the early work of Daniel Kahneman or Amos Tversky. They teamed, conducted experiments, and challenged the "rationality" of the economic person. In their work, they contended that people are hardwired for decision-making errors. Moreover, they suggested that people make suboptimal decisions, jeopardize their future, hurt their relationships, and do not always optimize their wealth. Since their groundbreaking work, there have been many insightful books on behavioral economics like *Nudge* by Thaler and Sunstein, *Freakonomics* by Levitt and Dubner, and *Predictably Irrational* by Dan Ariely. To that end, this resource introduces the reader to practice exercises on the intersection between behavioral economics and decision making.

Purpose

The purpose of this book is to provide leaders and leadership development professionals with exercises for effective decision making. The exercises in this book can

- act as team-building processes and help team members understand each other better;

- assist team members in discussing difficult topics and help them build understanding and appreciation of other people's cognitive processes

- help employees do an effective audit of decision-making practices used by their organizations.

About the Authors

Dr. Richard Brynteson   **(651) 246-3147 • brynteson@csp.edu**

"Richard will push your thinking." As an organizational consultant, executive coach, teacher, and writer, Richard helps his students and clients examine their own thinking and make changes in order to improve their productivity and quality of life. Richard helps his clients innovate work processes and products in order to improve effectiveness and efficiency. He helps his coaching clients explore the relevance of their own assumptions and paradigms. Richard shines a mirror at his coaching clients so they can see the flaws in their thinking. Dr. Brynteson has helped the Singapore military redesign work systems around Chinook helicopters, F-16 fighter planes, and Naval patrol boats. Richard has created leadership training programs for several companies. He has helped engineers become more personable, executives become less fearful, and managers become more thoughtful.

Representative Clients

- Department of Defense, Singapore
- Dell Computers, Malaysia
- McCann Erickson, Singapore and Kuala Lumpur
- Rochester Public Utilities
- Austin Utilities
- Healtheast
- Zumbro Valley Mental Health Centers
- Firstmark Services
- Medtronic, Anoka County

Professional Background

- Professor of Organizational Management, Concordia University (current)
- Innovation Consultant, Singapore and Kuala Lumpur
- Ecolab, Product Line Manager
- Software Clearing House, Marketing Manager
- W. R. Grace, Marketing Manager and Financial Analyst

Education

- University of Minnesota, Ph.D., Adult Education, 1997
- University of Chicago, MBA, Finance and Marketing, 1980
- Dartmouth College, BA, English, 1977

Publications

- *Once Upon a Complex Time: Using Stories to Understand Systems,* 2006, www.sparrowhawkmedia.com
- *The Manager's Pocket Guide to Innovation,* 2010, HRD Press
- *The Manager's Pocket Guide to Social Media,* 2011, HRD Press (with Carol Rinkoff and Jason DeBoer Moran)
- *The Manager's Guide to Behavioral Economics,* 2014, HRD Press

Dr. Steve Manderscheid

(612) 423-9783 • manderscheid@csp.edu

"Steve is a true practitioner at heart." Steve has twenty years of experience and a diverse background working with business leaders on organization and leadership development initiatives in several large and small national and international organizations. Steve works with clients to find the right solutions that have real positive financial impact. Steve challenges his clients to look past quick fix solutions and identify changes that will be effective in the short and long term. Steve has conducted academic program audits and facilitated talent management workshops in the Ukraine. He has also facilitated strategic planning and leadership development workshop in several industries, including nonprofit.

Representative Clients

- Truth Hardware
- Augsburg College
- Apogee, Inc.
- Digital River
- 3M
- The St. Paul
- Empak, Inc.
- Liberty Diversified Industries
- Techies.com
- Connect Computer
- RCRI
- Norstan, Inc.
- Degussa
- Volunteers of America
- Federal Reserve Bank
- Allina
- SHRM
- Nelson Building and Development
- Minnesota Board of Medical Practice
- hrconnection
- Kyiv Mohyla Business School— Ukraine

Professional Background

- Professor of Human Resource Management, Concordia University (current)
- Principal Consultant (Alchemy Consulting)
- Norstan Communication, Manager of Human Resource Development
- Liberty Diversified Industry, Sr. Training and Organization Development Consultant
- Empak, Training and Development Specialist
- 3M, Training and Development Fellow

Education

- University of St. Thomas, Ed.D., Organization Development, 2005
- University of Minnesota, M.Ed., Human Resource Development, 1994
- St. Cloud State University, Science of Technology, 1990

Publications

- Manderscheid, S., & Freeman, P. (2012). Polarity management and leadership transition. *The European Journal of Training and Development, 36*(9).

- Manderscheid, S., & Ardichvili, A. (2008). New leader assimilation: process and outcomes. *Leadership and Organization Development Journal, 29*(7-8), 661-677.

- Ardichvili, A., & Manderscheid, S. (2008—Issue Editor). Emerging practices in leadership development. *Advances in Human Resource Development, 10*(5).

- Ardichvili, A., & Manderscheid, S. (2008). Emerging Practices in Leadership Development: An Introduction. Advances in Human Resource Development, 10(5), 619-631.

- Manderscheid, S. (2008). New Leader Assimilation: An Intervention for Leaders in Transition. Advances in Human Resource Development, 10(5), 686-702.

- Manderscheid, S., & Ardichvili, A. (October, 2008). A Model for Leadership Transition. In Rozanski, A., Kuchinke, K. P., & Boyar, E. (Eds). (in press). Rozwoj zasobow ludzkich—teoria i praktyka [Human Resource Development—theory and practice]. Lublin, Poland: Lublin Technical University.

- Manderscheid, S., & Ardichvili, A. (2008). A conceptual model of leadership transition. *Performance Improvement Quarterly, 20*(3-4), 113-129.

- Manderscheid, S., & Kusy, M. (2004). How to design strategy with no dust—just results! *Organization Development Journal, 23*(2), 63-70.

Unit 1:
Decision-Making Basics

1 System 1/System 2 Basics

Story   I see it too often. A group of teens stands around for 20 minutes figuring out what to order at McDonald's. "Should I get a Happy Meal #3 with double fries?" These same teens probably have not thought for 20 minutes about how they could be of value to the community.

Concept   System 1 thinking: experiential, effortless, automatic, fast, opaque, intuitive, highly emotional, "fast and frugal." It produces heuristics or fast and dirty shortcuts.

System 2 thinking: reasoned, slower, logical, serial, progressive, reflective

We use both System 1 and System 2 thinking; both kinds are appropriate. We get into trouble when we mix them up. We might be rash for important decisions, or we might spend hours trying to decide which movie to watch.

Goal   The goal of this exercise is for teams to understand their decision-making process and agree on which decisions are System 1 and which are System 2.

Time   60 minutes

Materials   Flipchart and markers

Procedure   1. Select a group that works together and makes decisions together.

2. Discuss the definitions of System 1 and System 2 and give them examples. For instance, stopping at a red light or putting on a seat belt should be System 1 decisions. Buying a house or having a child should be System 2 decisions.

3. Put two pieces of flipchart paper up on the wall. Label one "System 1" and the other one "System 2."

4. Have the group brainstorm which kinds of decisions they make that should go under each heading. You may use consensus or voting if there is disagreement.

Debrief   Some questions that may create interesting discussions include:

1. How much agreement is there on these decisions?

2. Which kinds of decisions are hardest to classify?

3. Did this conversation help you understand each other better?

4. Who else should be brought in on this conversation?

Personal Application   Can you do this exercise with your family members? Which kinds of decisions are hardest to classify?

2 Decision Maker's Dilemma

Story
A leader is confronted with three equally appealing choices:

1. take a 10% increase in pay over the next calendar year,
2. have every other Friday off for the next calendar year, or
3. work virtually from San Diego during the winter months.

Concept
When the outcomes of two or more seemingly equal decisions are present, it can be difficult for decision makers to see the negative aspects of each decision. The decision maker is essentially blinded by the desirable outcomes of each choice. In some instances, the decision maker's inability to weigh the negative outcomes creates a situation where they become paralyzed with "no decision" as the final decision.

Goal
The goal of this exercise is to recognize dilemmas in decision making and further articulate and evaluate the downsides of each decision.

Time
30–40 minutes

Materials
Flipchart or whiteboard and markers

Procedure
1. Provide the example of a decision-making dilemma highlighted in the Story above.
2. Ask participants to work in groups of three to five and identify a decision-making dilemma.
3. Ask groups to share their decision-making dilemma. Write each group's dilemma on a flipchart or whiteboard and evaluate it to ensure that each group has a valid decision-making dilemma.
4. Instruct each group to discuss their decision-making dilemma and identify at least three drawbacks to each of the decision choices. After they have determined the cons of each decision choice, have the groups make their final decision.
5. After the groups work for 15 minutes, ask each group to restate their decision-making dilemma with the large group and share their final decision with a strong rationale.

Debrief
Some questions that may create interesting discussions include:

1. Was it difficult to identify a decision-making dilemma? If so, why?
2. What creates paralysis in the decision-making process?
3. What is the value in identifying the drawbacks of each potential choice?
4. Did identifying drawbacks help in making a final decision with a relatively strong rationale?

Exercise 2 (concluded)

Personal Application

How do you know when you are caught between two or more equally desirable decisions? What are personal cues and clues? Whom can you ask to help you explore the negatives of each of your decision choices?

3 | Choices and Criteria

Story
A leader is faced with deciding between several candidates to fill an important vacant position on their team. The leader has four top candidates and several important criteria to use for their evaluation. A helpful tool for the leader to use when evaluating each candidate on defined criteria is called the Measured Criteria Worksheet.

Concept
When making decisions, leaders need a process for evaluating several options before making a final decision. Often, those options are evaluated using well-defined criteria. By creating a simple Measured Criteria Worksheet like the examples on the following page that is specific to your decision criteria, leaders can organize choices and criteria for insightful and efficient decision making.

Goal
The goal of this exercise is to help leaders organize choices and criteria to make the best decisions efficiently.

Time
30 minutes

Materials
Paper and pens

Procedure
1. Explain to participants that leaders often need to make choices among various options using defined criteria; there can be any number of choices and criteria. Some criteria may have a value (i.e., cost), other criteria may be noted as "Yes" or "No," and some criteria can be ranked on a scale of 1 to 10.

2. Provide participants with at least one simple example that everyone can relate to (see worksheet examples on the following page).

3. Ask participants to identify an important decision they need to make that has multiple choices and defined criteria. Instruct them to develop a worksheet similar to the examples you shared. Encourage them to develop specific criteria and a scale for their criteria if they will be ranking the criteria (see Financial Acumen in the Select a New Team Member worksheet on the following page).

4. In the large work group, ask some participants to share a few examples from their worksheet. Moreover, ask them to provide reflections on the process of creating the worksheet.

Exercise 3 (concluded)

Purchase a Sport Utility Vehicle

Choice/ Criteria	Price (loaded)	Fuel Economy (city/highway)	Horsepower	Towing
Honda CRV	$28,540	24/27	210	1,500 lbs.
Ford Escape	$27,546	26/29	190	1,500 lbs.
Mazda CX5	$26,324	31/29	185	2,000 lbs.
Toyota RAV4	$29,789	25/30	200	1,500 lbs.

Select a New Team Member

Rating scale for financial acumen:

1 = limited ability to manage a project budget

10 = managed a project budget in excess of 10 million

Choice/ Criteria	PMI Certified	3–5 Years of Leadership Experience	Financial Acumen
Yolanda	Yes	No (1 year)	7
Charlie	No	Yes	10
Nyguen	Yes	Yes	9
Michelle	Yes	No (2 years)	5

Debrief Some questions that might create interesting discussions include:

1. Can you articulate some challenges associated with identifying criteria?

2. Is it possible to have too many criteria? If so, how might you prioritize?

Personal Application How can you incorporate this into your decision-making processes? How will you identify your criteria ?

4 Five Decision-Making Modes

Story

A leader expresses to her team that she would like to make a consensus decision. The leader then solicits feedback from the team and makes the decision on her own. The next time the leader attempts to make a consensus decision, the group appears apathetic. When the team was asked why they were "low energy" during a team meeting, one team member expressed, "I thought we were going to make a consensus (team) decision, not provide the leader with feedback for her to make the decision on her own."

Concept

Leaders need to be clear on the decision approach when working with teams. Leaders need to differentiate decision approaches and use an approach that yields the best decision with collective support.

Goal

The goal of this exercise is to have leaders differentiate between decision approaches and further select an approach that is most effective for each decision.

Time

30 minutes

Materials

PowerPoint Slide 4.1, flipchart or whiteboard, and markers

Procedure

1. Display Slide 4.1 or a prepared flipchart page with the following decision approaches. Explain each approach and suggest that leaders can benefit from understanding and articulating a decision approach to their teams.

   - **Unilateral** – The leader makes the decision on his own with no feedback from others.

   - **Consult and Decide** – The leader solicits feedback from his team and makes the decision on his own. The leader may or may not provide a rationale to the team.

   - **Build Consensus** – The team makes the decision together. The decision is one that everyone can support. It may not be the most preferred by every team member.

   - **Unanimous** – The team is in 100% agreement.

> - **Unilateral** – The leader makes the decision on his/her own with no feedback from others.
> - **Consult and Decide** – The leader solicits feedback from his/her team and makes the decision on his/her own. The leader may or may not provide a rationale to the team.
> - **Build Consensus** – The team makes the decision together. The decision is one that everyone can support. It may not be the most preferred by every team member.
> - **Unanimous** – The team is in 100% agreement.
>
> 4.1

Exercise 4 (concluded)

2. Ask participants to work in groups and identify the circumstances under which each of these approaches is most appropriate.

3. Ask each group to share their insights and capture a list of key criteria for each approach on a flipchart or whiteboard.

4. Explain that leaders should consider these criteria when determining a decision approach:

   a. Is team commitment important?

   b. Do I have enough information on my own to make the decision?

   c. Will others buy-in if I make the decision on my own?

   d. Is team conflict over the decision likely?

Debrief   Some questions that might create interesting discussions include:

1. What decision mode is most common in your organization?

2. What can leaders do in your organization to ensure that they use the most appropriate decision mode?

Personal Application   Do you use one decision-making mode in most situations? If so, how will you remind yourself to consider other modes?

5 The Great Paradox of Decision Making

Story
A leader needs to choose between two vendors with equal qualifications. The leader is unable to decide between both choices. Every day the leader delays the decision, it will cost the organization $20,000. The leader has consulted several colleagues who are close to the issue and none of them has been able to sway their opinion each way.

Concept
When leaders are faced with two equally appealing choices, they sometimes become paralyzed, and they unnecessarily delay important decisions. The following quote illustrates the paradox:

> *A man, being just as hungry as thirsty, and placed in between food and drink, must necessarily remain where he is and starve to death.*

> — Aristotle, *On the Heavens*, ca.350 BCE

Goal
The goal of this exercise is to help leaders recognize when they are trapped between two appealing choices. Moreover, the goal is to provide a few different frameworks to help leaders work through the paradox.

Time
20 minutes

Materials
PowerPoint Slide 5.1, flipchart, and markers

Procedure
1. Display Slide 5.1 showing a picture of a donkey standing between a bucket of water and a stack of hay. Explain to participants that the great paradox in decision making is when they are trapped between two equally appealing choices.

2. Ask participants to share some ways leaders might break out of the paradox, e.g., seek feedback from others.

3. Explain to participants that one way to break the paradox is to assemble a group of stakeholders and brainstorm all the potential downsides of each alternative.

4. Develop a simple T-chart on a piece of flipchart paper and provide an example familiar to participants (see example below). Explain that the decision maker can also ask stakeholders to assign a ranking for each of the items (1 = very negative to 10 = slightly negative). Each column can then be totaled for a final summary.

Exercise 5 (concluded)

VENDOR A (Kelly's Beauty Supply)	VENDOR B (Samuel's Beauty Now)
Limited high-end product selection (8)	High products priced above market (9)
Bi-weekly delivery (4)	Monthly delivery (3)
High-priced special orders (3)	No special orders (2)
etc.	etc.

Debrief

Some questions that might create interesting discussions include:

1. Is it possible for two choices to be equal?

2. What other strategies can one use to decide between two equally appealing choices. **Hint:** Think about including others in your analysis.

3. Can a decision maker list all the positives of each choice and get the same result? Try it.

Personal Application

Do you often have trouble deciding between choices? If so, you might want to consider using your intuition. Conduct no formal analysis and make a choice; wait one day and do an analysis and see if your result is similar. If it is similar, you might want to trust your intuition more.

6 Values and Decisions

Story Jerry finds himself procrastinating when attempting to make tough decisions. He does not feel like he has a solid foundation or framework to make important decisions. At times, he experiences a strong dissonance after making decisions. His decisions seem to be in conflict with his core beliefs.

Concept Values are the foundation of our decisions. If you would like to make better decisions, it is imperative that you understand how values guide your decision.

Goal The goal of this exercise is to help leaders understand how all decisions are reflections of their values.

Time 45 minutes

Materials PowerPoint Slides 6.1a and 6.1b

Procedure
1. Explain that values are tenets in life that are most important to you. They serve as a foundation for making important decisions.

2. Share the few common values below on Slides 6.1a and 6.1b (see thumbnails below) or on a flipchart:

   - **Integrity** – Maintaining a congruity between what one claims to be and how one acts
   - **Loyalty** – Seeking to be faithful, constant, and steadfast
   - **Competition** – Matching efforts or abilities with self or others
   - **Physical Fitness & Health** – Healthy regard for one's body, enjoying sports involvement
   - **Achievement** – Enjoying a sense of accomplishment
   - **Security** – Feeling safe and confident about the future
   - **Independence** – Wanting control of own time, behavior, and tasks
   - **Family** – Placing importance on maintaining familial relationships
   - **Friendship** – Placing importance on close, personal relationships

> **Integrity** – Maintaining a congruity between what one claims to be and how one acts
> **Loyalty** – Seeking to be faithful, constant, and steadfast
> **Competition** – Matching efforts or abilities with self or others
> **Physical Fitness & Health** – Healthy regard for one's body, enjoying sports involvement
> **Achievement** – Enjoying a sense of accomplishment

6.1a

> **Security** – Feeling safe and confident about the future
> **Independence** – Wanting control of own time, behavior, and tasks
> **Family** – Placing importance on maintaining familial relationships
> **Friendship** – Placing importance on close, personal relationships

6.1b

Exercise 6 (concluded)

3. Ask participants to make a list of 10 values that are important to them. Ask them to rank those values from 1 to 10, with 1 being the most important.

4. Map your values to three specific important decisions you have made in the past one to three years. Highlight the value(s), give an example, and explain the outcome.

5. Ask participants to be prepared to explain how their values served as a foundation for their decision making.

6. Debrief the activity in the large group.

Debrief   Some questions that might create interesting discussions are:

1. How can people be sure their values are congruent with their decisions?

2. Does this concept of linking values to decisions apply to stated corporate values and individual decision making?

3. How can leaders help individuals use their personal values and corporate values as a foundation to decision making?

Personal Application   Are you happy with how you live your values? Do you have some values you aspire to incorporate into your life? Either way, when you are challenged to make an ethical decision, be sure to reflect on your lived and aspired values.

7 Concerns to Clear Objectives

Story

A leader agonizes over making decisions because she can see only the issues. She is unable to move beyond articulating her concerns. The leader's concerns are clear; however, her objectives are not. Without clear objectives, the leader is not able to confirm the problem and evaluate alternatives.

Concept

Decisions are often a result of being dissatisfied with a current state. To that end, concerns can be a basis for identifying important objectives, which form the basis for evaluating alternatives.

> *The majority see the obstacles; the few see the objectives; history records the successes of the latter, while oblivion is the reward of the former.*
>
> – Alfred A. Montapert

Goal

The goal of this exercise is to help decision makers identify the most important factors when making a decision. The intent is to help decision makers evaluate and revise objectives based on core concerns.

Time

20 minutes

Materials

PowerPoint Slide 7.1; paper and pens

Procedure

1. Explain to participants that concerns are often a catalyst for making decisions. Explain that concerns can serve as a valuable foundation for identifying and clarifying objectives.

2. Show Slide 7.1 and provide participants an example of "Concerns to Objectives."

Concern–Objective Chart

CONCERN	OBJECTIVE
Driving the kids to school is time consuming and costly.	Live within five miles of the middle school.
Living near a busy road is a safety hazard for the kids.	Live on a quiet street that is free from busy traffic.
Family members have little to no privacy.	Increase the square footage of our living space by at least 1,000 sf.
The neighbors are upset with us for parking our boat in the street.	Etc...

7.1

3. Ask participants to construct a two-column table like the one shown in the slide and identify an important personal or professional decision they are considering.

4. Next, have participants identify at least 5 to 8 concerns and develop one clear objective (with an action verb) for each concern.

Exercise 7 (concluded)

5. Ask participants to share their decision at their table in small groups. Ask small group members to critique and question each member's decision and "Concern–Objective" table.

6. Make the following debriefing statements: (1) state that key concerns are often an effective foundation for gaining clarity on important objectives, (2) explain to participants that clear objectives serve as a basis for evaluating alternatives, (3) emphasize that articulating objectives helps ensure the right problem is stated and it drives additional steps in the decision-making process.

Debrief

The following question might create interesting discussions:

How can you make sure all of the most important concerns are articulated?

Personal Application

Do you get overwhelmed with concerns and find it difficult to make decisions? If so, develop a table before making important decisions.

8 Working with Polarity

Story George becomes conflicted easily when presented with decisions that do not have a clear choice. He often vacillates between both. George is not seeing the polarity: two interdependent poles (choices). Since he does not recognize polarities that need to be managed, he often swings on the pendulum between both choices; e.g., focus on work AND focus on home.

Concept According to Barry Johnson, there are problems to be solved and polarities that need to be managed. In some situations, decision makers need to choose between one or more alternatives. In other situations, they are faced with a polarity. Polarities are two interdependent poles that need to be managed overtime. To that end, a focus on work and home is a polarity. Moreover, inhaling and exhaling is a polarity. One cannot choose between one or the other; one must find a way to do both.

Goal The goal of this exercise is to help decision makers differentiate between decisions that need to be made and polarities that need to be managed. Moreover, the goal is to help decision makers develop a polarity map that will help them manage polarities over time.

Time 45 minutes

Materials Paper and pens

Procedure 1. Explain the concept of polarity and decision making. Provide examples of decisions that need to be made and polarities that need to be managed.

   Decisions to be made: Should I choose vendor A, B, or C? Should I move my family to Florida for a new position?

   Polarity to manage: work and home, organization change, stability, etc.

2. Ask participants to draw a four-quadrant matrix on a sheet of paper.

3. Ask participants to place the poles of their polarity on each side of the four quadrants, e.g., place "Home" on one side and "Work" on the other.

4. Have participants further identify at least three upsides and downsides of focusing on each pole.

5. After they complete the matrix, ask participants to identify 3 to 5 specific actions they can take to drive the upsides of each of their poles (e.g., home and work). They should have a list for both poles.

6. Ask participants to identify 3 to 5 red flags for each pole. A red flag is a measurable indicator that they are focusing too much on one pole at the expense of the other.

7. Ask each participant to share and explain his or her polarity to the large group. Do this to share examples, confirm learning, and give an opportunity for others to provide feedback.

Exercise 8 (concluded)

Action Steps	1. Build a better relationship with children 2. 3.	1. Earn more money 2. 3.	Action Steps
	——— HOME ———	——— WORK ———	
Red Flags	1. Missed deadlines 2. 3.	1. Burnout and stress 2. 3.	Red Flags

8. Explain to participants that polarity maps are intended to be revisited and revised over time. Express that polarity maps can be developed with multiple stakeholders across an organization or they can be developed individually.

Debrief

Some questions that might create interesting discussions include:

1. What important polarities exist in your organization?

2. How might individuals in your organization respond to the process of mapping polarities?

3. Can you create a process where a polarity map is monitored over time?

Personal Application

What polarities exist in your personal and professional life? How can you be more effective by identifying and mapping polarities? What challenges exist for you?

9 Decision-Making Styles

Story　　Have you ever wondered why decision making is difficult for some teams and very easy for others? Some of this has to do with decision-making style. If everyone has the same approach to decision making, the process tends to be more fluid. If several team members have a very different approach, the process can be time consuming and a bit agonizing.

Concept　　If we can identify the decision-making styles (tendencies) of other team members, it can be less challenging to come to agreement on an approach for making decisions.

Goal　　The intent is not to assemble a team of like-minded people for decision making; the intent is to acknowledge the differences in others and develop the best approach to ensure a decision is made in a timely and effective manner.

Time　　30 minutes

Materials　　PowerPoint Slides 9.1a and 9.1b; flipchart or whiteboard and markers

Procedure

1. Explain to participants that everyone has their own decision-making style. Provide an overview of four relatively common styles. Express that these are not perfect categories that describe everyone. Participants may or may not find themselves in one of the categories.

2. Show PowerPoint Slides 9.1a and 9.1b (see thumbnails on the next page) or write the following different decision-making styles on a flipchart page and review with participants:

   - **Rational decision makers** – These individuals are process oriented. They typically tend to drive toward having a definite process for decision making.

   - **Analytical decision makers** – These individuals tend to collect a lot of data before making decisions. They typically want as much information as possible before making a decision.

   - **Personable decision makers** – These individuals are usually focused on the perspective of others. They typically want to involve others in decision making or at least consider their perspectives.

   - **Global decision makers** – These individuals seek possibilities. They typically want to get all the possibilities out in the open before making a decision.

Exercise 9 (concluded)

<table>
<tr>
<td>

Rational decision makers are process oriented; typically tend to drive toward having a definite process for decision making

Analytical decision makers tend to collect a lot of data before making decisions; typically want as much information as possible before making a decision

9.1a
</td>
<td>

Personable decision makers are usually focused on the perspective of others; typically want to involve others in decision making or at least consider their perspectives

Global decision makers seek possibilities; typically want to get all possibilities out in the open before making a decision

9.1b
</td>
</tr>
</table>

3. Ask participants to share the advantages and disadvantages of each style and facilitate a discussion. **Option:** Ask groups to work in small groups to process advantages and disadvantages.

4. Place the matrix shown below on a whiteboard or flipchart page. Ask each participant to write their name in the quadrant that best describes their style.

Rational	**Analytical**
Personable	**Global**

Debrief   Some questions that might create interesting discussions include:

1. What does the decision profile of participants (see matrix) tell you about the team's decision-making style?

2. Why is it important to understand decision styles of team members?

3. How can understanding decision styles help a team make better decisions?

4. What can teams do to understand decision styles?

Personal Application   What can you do to understand your style? What approach can you take to identify the style of others? Are there ways you can be more flexible with your approach to decision making?

10 Event, Pattern, and Structure

Story
Joe is late for work on Friday; this is an event. Joe is always late for work on Fridays; this is a pattern. Joe is late for work on Fridays because he gets paid on Thursday nights and uses a portion of his paycheck to support his gambling addiction; gambling addiction may be the structure.

Concept
Decision makers should not react to single events. They should look for patterns and the underlying cause of events before taking action. If they can see the event, they are able to react. If they can see the pattern, they can anticipate. If they understand the structure, they can make an effective decision to influence the pattern and subsequent events.

Goal
The goal of this exercise is to help decision makers recognize events (tip of the iceberg), patterns, and most importantly structures (iceberg underwater). If they can see the relationship of all three, they will be better equipped to make effective decisions.

Time
30 minutes

Materials
Event, Pattern, and Structure Worksheet and pens

Procedure
1. Explain the event, pattern, and structure concept. Provide one personal or professional example from your own experience (see Story above).

2. Distribute the Event, Pattern, and Structure Worksheet.

3. Ask participants to identify two examples that fit the Event, Pattern, and Structure model. Encourage participants to identify one personal and one professional example.

4. After 10 minutes, ask two or three participants to share their examples.

5. Debrief in the large group.

Debrief
Some questions that might create interesting discussions include:

1. Was it easy to identify and clarify the relationship between event, pattern, and structure? If not, what was challenging?

2. How might you use this model to be a more effective decision maker?

Personal Application
Use the worksheet to help you look more deeply at recurring issues. After you practice, you will begin to see patterns and structure more easily.

Event, Pattern, and Structure Worksheet

EVENT
1. _____
_____
2. _____
_____

PATTERN
1. _____
_____
2. _____
_____

STRUCTURE
1. _____
_____
2. _____
_____

Unit 2:
Behavioral Economics Principles

11 Default Settings

Story   In a study conducted several years ago, it was found that half of the European countries had over 90% participation in organ donation. The other half of the countries had fewer than 20% participation. What was the difference? The high compliance countries had "opt-in" participation as the default in the DMV (Department of Motor Vehicles) forms. The low participation countries had "opt-out" as the default.

Concept   The default setting is powerful. Be careful what you set as the default box.

Goal   The goal of this exercise is to help participants see what unseen "default" settings exist in their organization.

Time   30–60 minutes

Materials   Pens; organizational literature

Procedure   1. Before the session, assemble internal and external organizational communications: HR forms, customer service websites, sales websites, etc.

2. Assemble a work group of 5–10 employees.

3. Explain the concept of defaults. Explain how people pick defaults naturally, without a thought. Ask the question: "How can our organization benefit from defaults?"

4. Have participants work through the assembled literature. The first step would be to identify when internal or external customers can choose a default box. The second step would be to discuss what alternative defaults might be.

Debrief   Some questions that might create interesting discussions include:

1. Let us laugh at ourselves. When have we selected the default option when it was not in our best interests? Such as accepted an invitation for three free copies of a magazine and then forget to cancel it? Such as boxes in HR benefit forms? Such as any government forms?

2. What organizations do you know of that use the default option effectively?

3. What default options could be created by your organization?

4. How could you raise awareness in your organization of default options?

Personal Application   When do you and your family use the default option? When is it to your advantage and not to your advantage?

12 Loss Aversion

Story

People were asked if they would opt in for a surgery that has a 70% success rate. Another group of people were asked if they would have a surgery that failed 30% of the time. Far more people in the first group responded positively.

Which of the following would you choose?

    a.   10% chance to win $95 and 90% chance of losing $5

    b.   Pay $5 to enter lottery where there is 10% chance to win $100 and a 90% chance to win $0

A large majority of people would choose (b). Yet, the two options are equal. Why did we choose (b)? We hate the idea of loss. Paying a fee is easily palatable, but losing $5 is hard to take. Study after study—whether in gambling, money, or other items—showed the same result: people avoid losses at all costs.

Concept

People are loss averse. They wish to avoid loss whenever possible.

Goal

The goal of this exercise is to have a work group (e.g., marketing, sales) examine the offerings of an organization to see where potential customers might have reservations about potential losses.

Time

30–60 minutes

Materials

Flipchart, pens, organization sales policies

Procedure

1. Before the session, assemble documentation of the organization's sales policies.

2. Assemble a work group of 5–10 employees.

3. Explain the concept of loss aversion. Ask for examples.

4. Have participants use the organization's sales policies to examine the process of buying from or using the services from your organization. Where are potential losses? Where might the buyer be potentially frozen in fright?

5. Make a list on a flipchart of those "fear of loss" places. How could your organization remedy these through changing of policies?

Debrief

Some questions that might create interesting discussions include:

1. When are you most loss averse? When does fear of loss creep into your feelings?

2. When might a potential client/customer have fears in doing business with you?

3. Are there small places and large places where fear of loss exists?

4. How can you create policies or literature to placate these fears of loss?

Personal Application

When do you feel big fears of loss? Are they rational? What do you do about them?

13 Expert Intuition

Story

Several economists have analyzed returns of stock analysts and financial planners. Their results indicate that these "experts" generally do no better than the market itself. Nobel Prize winner Daniel Kahneman suggests that this is because intuition can only be trusted in a predictable environment where there is an opportunity for prolonged practice. Examples of where intuition would work are the games of chess, bridge, and poker. The stock market and politics do not operate in stable, regular environments. Emotion and unforeseen events often dictate results in these environments.

Concept

Trusting intuition can work only in stable environments where prolonged practice is available.

Goal

The goal of this exercise is for participants to more deeply understand the uses and limits of their own intuitions.

Time

60 minutes

Materials

Stable/Unstable Environment Worksheet and pens

Procedure

1. Assemble a group of 5–10 participants.
2. Discuss or read the Story above. Discuss the concept of intuition.
3. Distribute the Stable/Unstable Environment Worksheet.
4. Have the small groups think about and discuss situations where the environment is more stable and less stable and where practice time is available or not.
5. Have participants fill in the quadrants with decision-making situations.

Debrief

Some questions that might create interesting discussions include:

1. If your intuition is not developed in an area, what might you do? (gather data)
2. Can you always discriminate well between stable and unstable environments?
3. How can you make time/space for practice when you wish to develop your intuition?
4. How do we admit to what we do not know and still save face?

Personal Application

Where do you have the practice to make for a good intuition? Where would you like to have it?

Stable/Unstable Environment Worksheet

Think about and discuss situations where the environment is more stable and less stable and where practice time is available or not. Then fill in the quadrants with decision-making situations.

Stable/Practiced	**Unstable/Practiced**
Stable/Unpracticed	**Unstable/Unpracticed**

14 | What drives you?

Story   Daniel Pink, the author of *Drive*, synthesizes research on motivation. He suggests that while monetary compensation might be effective for mechanical and physical tasks (factory assembly, digging, etc.), it is not the best motivator for "knowledge" work. His research suggests that purpose, mastery, and autonomy are better motivators for that kind of work.

Concept   Our ideas about motivation may be outdated and even counter-productive. We need to find new ways to motivate knowledge workers.

Goal   The goal of this exercise is to have participants examine the incentives of their organization and look for other ways to incent employees.

Time   1–2 hours

Materials   Drive Worksheet; flipchart and markers

Procedure

1. Assemble a team from your organization that is interested in motivators and incentives.

2. On flipchart paper, create two columns labeled "Monetary Incentives" and "Proof that It Works."

3. Facilitate creation of a list of monetary or monetary-like incentives, which the organization employs.

4. Have the group evaluate any evidence that suggests that these incentives work to achieve the desired goals. Look for hard evidence as well as anecdotal evidence.

5. Distribute the Drive Worksheet to participants. Show the RSA Animate Drive YouTube (Drive, Dan Pink, 10 minutes long).

6. Have participants brainstorm ways of creating motivation with Purpose, Autonomy, and Mastery within the organization and document their ideas on the worksheet.

Debrief   Some questions that might create interesting discussions include:

1. Who else needs to be brought in on this conversation?

2. What other conversations need to happen around motivation?

3. What are the best motivators in this organization?

4. How can we increase purpose, mastery, and autonomy in this organization?

Personal Application   What really motivates you to get out of bed in the morning? How can you get more of this?

Drive Worksheet

Drive Factor	Possible Organizational Motivators
Purpose	
Autonomy	
Mastery	

15 Monkeys and Empathy

Story

Daniel Goleman, in *Social Intelligence,* tells the story about a monkey experiment. Groups of monkeys are trained that if they pull a lever, they will receive food. However, a monkey in another room screams when they pull the food lever. If they pull the lever more softly, it hurts the other monkey less, but they get less food. Most monkeys pull the lever more softly in order to reduce the pain of the other monkey. A couple of monkeys, however, quit pulling the lever at all and slowly starve themselves. They do not want to do harm to the other monkey at all.

Concept

Sometimes, we shoot ourselves in the foot in order to help the customer. We have developed such a culture of customer service that we neglect the organization's needs to stay viable.

Goal

The goal of this exercise is to help participants see where they might be neglecting their company's needs for the needs of the customers.

Time

30–60 minutes

Materials

Flipchart and markers

Procedure

1. Assemble a group or team.

2. Discuss the concept of empathy:
   a. How it helps customer service
   b. How it is part of emotional intelligence
   c. How it can improve employee relationships
   d. How it can help in coaching others

3. Look at the "dark side" of empathy and document the group's answers to the questions below on a flipchart:
   a. When do we, as an organization, do as the monkeys do and hurt ourselves because of our empathy?

   b. Are there clients that require too much time and are not worth the trouble?

   c. Are there customers we should fire because they cost too much?

   d. When do we put too much energy in carrying certain employees even when they are not productive?

   e. Are we poisoning ourselves because of a few unprofitable pet projects or product lines?

Exercise 15 (concluded)

Debrief

Some questions that might create interesting discussions include:

1. When do we, as an organization, do as the monkeys do and hurt ourselves because of our empathy?

2. Are there clients that require too much time and are not worth the trouble?

3. Are there customers we should fire because they cost too much?

4. When do we put too much energy in carrying certain employees even when they are not productive?

5. Are we poisoning ourselves because of a few unprofitable pet projects or product lines?

Personal Application

When are you poisoning/hurting yourself for the sake of others? When does it become a point of diminishing returns for a certain project?

16 The Elephant, the Rider, and the Path

Story   Heath and Heath, in *Switch*, write that getting things done takes a combination of three elements: the rider, the elephant, and the path. One needs to direct the rider (or the intellect), motivate the elephant (or the heart or emotions) that she is riding, and clear the path ahead of them. If one of these actions is missing, goals will not be reached.

Concept   The rider, the elephant, and the path are the three pieces that need to be in place in order to accomplish important things.

Goal   The goal of this exercise is to help participants understand the roles of the rider, elephant, and path in achieving personal and organizational goals.

Time   60 minutes

Materials   Switch Worksheet and pens

Procedure   1. Before the session, read excerpts from *Switch* in order to familiarize yourself with the concepts of the rider, elephant, and path.

                   2. Assemble a group of 5–10 employees who are working on a project or concept.

                   3. Explain the principles of *Switch.*

                   4. Distribute the Switch Worksheet and have the group work on one or two projects: how can they direct the rider, how can they motivate the elephant, and how can they clear the path?

Debrief   Some questions that might create interesting discussions include:

                   1. In this organization, when is the rider in charge? The elephant? The path?

                   2. How can you make the path easier for potential employees? Potential customers?

                   3. Who else needs to be a part of this conversation?

Personal Application   When are you poisoning/hurting yourself for the sake of others? When does it become a point of diminishing returns for a certain project?

Switch Worksheet

Piece	Concept/Project #1	Concept/Project #2
Rider		
Elephant		
Path		

17 Anchoring and Adjustment

Story Students were given two sets of numbers and told to quickly calculate these in their heads:

$$1 \times 2 \times 3 \times 4 \times 5 \times 6 \times 7 \times 8 = ?$$

and

$$8 \times 7 \times 6 \times 5 \times 4 \times 3 \times 2 \times 1 = ?$$

The results: For the first equation, the students' guesses averaged 512. For the second equation, the students' guesses averaged 2,250. As you can see, these two equations are equal (actual answer = 40,320). The students clearly anchored on the first couple of numbers and overemphasized these.

Concept We tend to anchor on the first bits of information and then make adjustments.

Goal The goal of this exercise is for participants to understand how anchoring and adjustment might work for them, their customers, and their suppliers.

Time 30 minutes

Materials Flipchart and markers

Procedure
1. Assemble a work group of 5 to 10 employees.
2. Ask participants to discuss the following questions:
   a. How is this organization anchored toward employees or clients?
   b. How are members of our organization anchored by others—such as salespeople, for instance?
3. Document their answers on the flipchart.

Debrief Some questions that might create interesting discussions include:
1. Students were told to write down the last four digits of their social security number and then bid on a bottle of wine. Those with higher social security numbers bid more for the wine than those with lower numbers. How might we fall into this trap?
2. How do we listen to others and then anchor on the first number we hear?

Personal Application How do you allow salespeople or your children to set anchor points for you? How can you be more conscious of this in the future?

18 Lowering Cognitive Effort

Story   At one point, I was refinancing my house. I was trying to figure out the myriad of forms that needed to be filled out. At a couple of points, I barked out "Do they really want my business?"

I like the formal clothes of a certain men's store. Yet their signage on pricing is very confusing. Many signs say "buy one, get one free," or "two for $135" but it is extremely difficult to discern which signs match which shirts or pants.

In both cases, I am using way too much cognitive effort. It is too difficult to do business with these organizations. Ultimately, I will find other places to do business.

Concept   Businesses need to lower the cognitive strain of customers and clients.

Goal   The goal of this exercise is to help participants raise their awareness of the cognitive strain that they place on customers or potential customers.

Time   60 minutes

Materials   Flipchart and markers

Procedure
1. Assemble a work group of 5 to 10 employees.
2. Map out the path that your customers (or potential customers) take in doing business with you on the flipchart.
   a. What steps do they go through?
   b. What are the critical junctures that your customers take in the process? At which junctures might you lose them? Where might they get confused? What step might be emotionally draining for them?
   c. How can you change these sticking points?

Debrief   Some questions that might create interesting discussions include:
1. Chipotle makes it easy. You go there if you want a burrito. Easy. Then, all you have to do is quickly decide if you want lettuce, onions, peppers, etc. How can you offer one thing, make the decision making easy, and keep the customers coming anyway?
2. Who else needs to be brought into this conversation?

Personal Application   When have you wanted more cognitive ease? How do companies that you deal with create cognitive ease?

19 Imposed Self-Control

Story
Social security, at its best, is an excellent way to impose retirement savings on the people of the United States. One Pakistani bank takes deposits from farmers during harvest time and does not release the funds until it is time for these parents to pay tuition to school for their children. Some Bangladesh farmers save in a locked box and only their neighbor has a key.

I have found that it does not make sense to keep ice cream in the freezer at home—I just eat it. It is easier not to have the temptation.

Concept
According to many experiments in behavioral economics, self-imposed discipline is very effective. Self-imposed deadlines, savings plans, and diet plans work better than loosey-goosey guidelines.

Goal
The goal of this exercise is for participants to practice thinking about self-imposed discipline and their clients/customers.

Time
30–60 minutes

Materials
None

Procedure
1. Assemble a work group that is interested in this subject.
2. Discuss ways imposed deadlines and constraints have been helpful in your lives. How has forced discipline been helpful in getting things done?
3. Discuss how your company/organization can help its clients with self-imposed discipline. Examples may include:
   a. $10 direct deposit for donations to your nonprofit church
   b. Taking a small amount out of a paycheck for investment or savings
   c. Forced savings through a layaway plan for future spending
   d. A warning note if certain mileposts are not met

Debrief
Some questions that might create interesting discussions include:
1. Can you be creative about imposing a discipline on customers without looking like you are controlling them?
2. Are there new ways of looking at imposing discipline as a gift and not a control mechanism?

Personal Application
What enforced discipline works in your life? The life of your family? What mechanisms would move your family toward its goals?

20 The Law of Unintended Consequences

Story

Meg loves dogs. She saw a stray one at the humane society and had to adopt it, despite the fact she already had two dogs. The veterinary bills of this new dog taxed her family, already living on the financial margins.

Everyone in the department loved Sammy even though he never quite was able to do his job. No one had the heart to let him go. Over the months, coworkers became more and more frustrated because they had to cover for Sammy, and much ill will ensued.

Concept

The law of unintentional consequences suggests that all of our decisions have consequences. In particular, emotional-based choices can have some very harsh consequences. It is best to try to predict those consequences ahead of time.

Goal

The goal of this exercise is to help participants understand the unintended consequences of their actions.

Time

60 minutes

Materials

Unintentional Consequences Worksheet and pens

Procedure

1. Assemble a work group of 5 to 20 employees who want to work together creating better decisions.

2. Talk about the law of unintentional consequences and its impact on our lives.

3. Using the Unintentional Consequences Worksheet, have the group look at past decisions, particularly those that had sub-optimal outcomes. The Unintentional Consequences Worksheet includes these columns:

   a. **Rational Pull:** Reasoning behind the choice you made.

   b. **Emotional Factors:** Which emotional factors were pulling you toward that decision?

   c. **Ongoing Impact on You:** What have been the unintentional consequences on you?

   d. **Ongoing Impact on Others:** What have been the unintentional consequences on others?

Debrief

Some questions that might create interesting discussions include:

1. What are some unintentional consequences of organizational policies?

2. Some unintentional consequences can be predicted; others cannot. How can you minimize those that cannot?

Personal Application

How does the law of unintentional consequences work in your life? What are some of the unintentional consequences (good or bad) of major decisions in your life?

Unintentional Consequences Worksheet

CHOICE	RATIONAL PULL	EMOTIONAL FACTORS	ONGOING IMPACT ON YOU	ONGOING IMPACT ON OTHERS

21 Value Attribution

Story   Dan Ariely writes about experiments in ownership and the endowment effect. People put more value on things they have bought than things they are given, or they not yet own. For instance, people were much more likely to drive through a snowstorm to go to a Duke basketball game if they bought the tickets rather than if they were given the tickets. People put a higher value on wall hangings that they already owned than ones that they did not own, even if these had the same value.

Concept   Emotionally, we overvalue things that we already own. "Actual" value means much less than our perceived, emotionally laden value.

Goal   The goal of this exercise is to help participants understand how they (and their organization) may be trapped by the endowment effect and may be overvaluing some of their assets.

Time   60 minutes

Materials   Flipchart or Endowment Effect Worksheet, markers, and pens

Procedure
1. Assemble a work group of 5 to 10 employees.
2. Explain to the group this endowment effect concept. Use examples from your own life. Another example of the endowment effect is Ikea. When you spend hours putting together your furniture, you tend to overvalue it.
3. Using the Endowment Effect Worksheet or a piece of flipchart paper, have the group(s) discuss various types of ownership and where the organization might overvalue some of its assets.

Debrief   Some questions that might create interesting discussions include:
1. How did the organization or individuals within the organization come to overvalue these assets?
2. Which of the perceived values are hardest to let go of? Why?
3. Are there organizational policies that could prevent overvaluing of assets in the future?
4. What are some of the costs of overvaluing assets? Time? Financial? Space? Re-work? Cumbersome systems? Chronic disagreements?

Personal Application   Where do you have a hard time letting go? What possessions or situations do you overvalue? How did it come to this?

Endowment Effect Worksheet

ASSET	CURRENT VALUE: Quanitative or Qualitative?	HOW DID IT BECOME OVERVALUED?	PROBABLE VALUE
Product			
Service			
Process			
Physical Space			
Market Segment			
Person			
Position			

22 Black Pearls

Story
Dan Ariely, in *Predictably Irrational*, tells the story about the marketing of black pearls. At first, the vendors could not sell them. When they were placed in windows next to high-end jewelry items, their perceived value skyrocketed and sales rose.

In other situations, retailers are successful in placing higher priced items next to items that they wish to sell. Buyers will not buy the highest priced items but will buy the next item, which is lower in price. Again, the context made the difference.

Concept
People see value in context not as an absolute. Products and services are sold with a context and not in a vacuum.

Goal
The goal of this exercise is for participants to understand that products and services are not viewed in the abstract but in the context of their surroundings.

Time
30–60 minutes

Materials
Context Worksheet and pens

Procedure
1. Assemble a team or teams of 6 to 8 people from your organization.
2. Discuss the research and concept of context with them.
3. Distribute the Context Worksheet. (**Note:** Not all the rows will fit for every situation.)
4. Historical context refers to how your organization has placed its products/services in the past.
5. Current context refers to how your products/services are currently displayed or placed. For instance,

   - Is your office in a grimy warehouse district?
   - Are your office workers dressed appropriately for the industry?
   - What stores or aisles are your products displayed in?
   - What competitors are you compared to?
   - How is your pricing compared to that of your competitors?
   - In which media are your advertisements placed?

6. Preferred context refers to where your products might be placed to increase their perceived value to the customer.

Exercise 22 (continued)

Debrief

Some questions that might create interesting discussions include:

1. As you shop, where do you see incongruities in context?

2. As you observe the world, where do you see incongruities in context?

3. What is the brand promise of your organization? Do all of your contexts promote that brand promise?

4. Which contexts in the worksheet do you find most incongruous? Least incongruous?

5. What steps can we take now to bridge these incongruities?

Personal Application

Who are your closest associates? Are they idea people? Are they people that others look up to? What music do you listen to? Upbeat or depressing?

Context Worksheet

"THING"	HISTORICAL CONTEXT	CURRENT CONTEXT	PREFERRED CONTEXT
Office Location			
Office Space			
Product Placement			
Service Placement			
Promotion Placement			
Other:			
Other:			

23 | You call this work?

Story   Tom Sawyer had to whitewash (paint) a fence, an onerous task on a hot day. Soon, he had his best friends doing the work while he supervised. He had convinced them that this was not "work" but a "privilege" and they were lucky to have such an opportunity.

Starbucks upgraded the image of coffee and calls it Italian, upscale sounding words. Their message: This is not just coffee; this is a venti macchiato. It is a privilege to be drinking it.

Concept   Tasks, products, services—almost everything—is framed by a context. Change the framing, or the context, and you will change the perceived value.

Goal   The goal of this exercise is to upgrade the image of tasks within the organization and to improve employee engagement.

Time   30–60 minutes

Materials   Whitewashing Worksheet and pens

Procedure
1. Assemble a work group of 6 to 8 employees.
2. Distribute the Whitewashing Worksheet.
3. Ask the group to list some organizational tasks that seem onerous, boring, or undesirable.
4. Have the group brainstorm ways to make those tasks more appealing, exciting, or fun to do.

Debrief   Some questions that might create interesting discussions include:

1. Do tasks have to necessarily be onerous or can they always be interesting? When a friend cleans her house, she allocates one room per long, upbeat song. The same person made lice-removal into a beauty night of cucumbers on the eyes, facial mud, and other beauty enhancements.

2. Making tasks interesting will raise employee engagement. With employee engagement in the United States at a very low point, raising employee engagement is an organizational imperative. What are other ways to make tasks more interesting?

3. What makes for interesting tasks for a Boomer? For an Xer? For a Millennial?

4. Good motivational theory suggests that management should provide the "what" and allow employees to provide the "how." To what extent does your organization do this? To what extent can it?

Personal Application   What jobs do you find onerous? How can you make them interesting?

Whitewashing Worksheet

TASK	CURRENT IMAGE	WAYS TO UPGRADE TASK OR IMAGE

24 Nice Words, Mean Words

Story Participants in a study were divided into two groups: one group read nice words, one group read mean words. Guess what? The ones who read the mean words behaved more abrasively than those who read the nice words. The same experiment was conducted with non-senior citizen type words and then senior citizen type (slow, deliberate, older, senior, aging) words. The subjects who read the words associated with seniors walked much more slowly after reading them.

Other studies have shown the same effect—what we read or hear can prime us for certain kinds of behavior.

Concept Priming is exposing a subject to a stimulus in order to alter his/her behavior in the future. Human beings can be primed to behave in certain ways by altering how we interact with them.

Goal The goal of this exercise is for participants to understand the concept of priming and apply it to their organization.

Time 60 minutes

Materials Corporate external and internal communication tools, paper, and pens

Procedure
1. Before the session, gather as much corporate literature as possible. These might include sales sheets, brochures, selling scripts, or the corporate website. You might include field notes of listening to your customer service reps or salespeople on the phone. What are they saying and how are they saying it?

2. Assemble one or more work groups of 4–8 people.

3. Explain the concept of priming. If further explanation is needed, pull up definitions and examples from Wikipedia or psychology textbooks.

4. Distribute literature to the groups and have them circle all negative words or connotations. Ask participants, "How can you word these more positively? Can you make clients/customers smile when they interact with you or your literature?"

Debrief Some questions that might create interesting discussions include:
1. Have you ever felt primed by salespeople? How?

2. Have you ever noticed people using extensive positive or extensive negative language? How does that impact you? Do you notice your own use of language in that way?

3. How could your own organization be more attentive and conscious of the language it uses? In which communication?

Personal Application In interacting with others, can you observe and monitor your own language usage, positive or negative?

25 Availability to the Imagination

Story

The authors of this book live in Minnesota. Some people in Minnesota are fearful of shark attacks on ocean beaches because these stand out in news stories. If you live in Minnesota, you are much more likely to be hurt by a deer hitting your car than a shark during your once-a-year visit to an ocean beach.

Likewise, some people dread air travel because of the publicity around rare air crashes. Again, one is much more likely to die in a car accident near home than in an airplane crash. However, air crashes are much more widely publicized.

Wikipedia defines the availability heuristic as:

> The availability heuristic is a mental shortcut that occurs when people make judgments about the probability of events by how easy it is to think of examples. The availability heuristic operates on the notion that if something can be recalled, it must be important.

Concept

People put much more credence in images that are palpable to the imagination and that can be recalled by memory.

Goal

The goal of this exercise is to audit your organization's communication and ascertain which elements are palpable to the imagination, using the principles of Heath and Heath's *Made to Stick*.

Time

60 minutes

Materials

Made to Stick Definitions, Availability through *Made to Stick* Principles Worksheet and pens

Procedure

1. Before the session, assemble some of your organization's communication tools: website pages, brochures, customer service routines.

2. Assemble a work group(s) that is familiar with your organization's product/service offerings and its communication strategies.

3. Distribute the *Made to Stick* worksheet and definitions and let participants read the definitions.

4. Have participants look over the organization's communication tools and apply the *Made to Stick* tools methodically. For instance, are the offerings "simple" enough for most people to understand? Do the advertisements have some "unexpected" aspect that will catch the attention of viewers?

Exercise 25 (continued)

Debrief

Some questions that might create interesting discussions include:

1. Are there gaps in your communication strategies?

2. Are there other communication tools where your organization can be more "available" to your potential customers?

3. Which of the six sticking methods has the most potential to make you more available? How?

4. What action steps would make it easier for your products or services to be more easily remembered?

Personal Application

How can you build your personal brand using the principles of *Made to Stick?*

Made to Stick Definitions

Chip Heath and Dan Heath

Principle 1: Simplicity

How do we find the essential core of our ideas? A successful defense lawyer says, "If you argue ten points, even if each is a good point, when they get back to the jury room they won't remember any." To strip an idea down to its core, we must be masters of exclusion. We must relentlessly prioritize. Saying something short is not the mission—sound bites are not the ideal. Proverbs are the ideal. We must create ideas that are both simple *and* profound. The Golden Rule is the ultimate model of simplicity: a one-sentence statement so profound that an individual could spend a lifetime learning to follow it.

Principle 2: Unexpectedness

How do we get our audience to pay attention to our ideas, and how do we maintain their interest when we need time to get the ideas across? We need to violate people's expectations. We need to be counterintuitive: "A bag of popcorn is as unhealthy as *a whole day's worth of fatty foods!*" We can use surprise—an emotion whose function is to increase alertness and cause focus—to grab people's attention. However, surprise doesn't last. For our idea to endure, we must generate *interest* and *curiosity.* How do you keep students engaged during the forty-eighth history class of the year? We can engage people's curiosity over a long period of time by systematically opening gaps in their knowledge and then filling those gaps.

Principle 3: Concreteness

How do we make our ideas clear? We must explain our ideas in terms of human actions, in terms of sensory information. This is where so much business communication goes awry. Mission statements, synergies, strategies, visions: they are often ambiguous to the point of being meaningless. Naturally, sticky ideas are full of concrete images—ice-filled bathtubs, apples with razors—because our brains are wired to remember concrete data. In proverbs, abstract truths are often encoded in concrete language: "A bird in the hand is worth two in the bush." Speaking concretely is the only way to ensure that our idea will mean the same thing to everyone in our audience.

Principle 4: Credibility

How do we make people believe our ideas? When the former surgeon general C. Everett Koop talks about a public-health issue, most people accept his ideas without skepticism. Nevertheless, in most day-to-day situations, we do not enjoy this authority. Sticky ideas have to carry their own credentials. We need ways to help people test our ideas for themselves—a "try before you buy" philosophy for the world of ideas. When we are trying to build a case for something, most of us instinctively grasp for hard numbers. However, in many cases this is exactly the wrong approach. In the sole U.S. presidential debate in 1980 between Ronald Reagan and Jimmy Carter, Reagan could have cited innumerable statistics demonstrating the sluggishness of the economy. Instead, he asked a simple question that allowed voters to test for themselves: "Before you vote, ask yourself if you are better off today than you were four years ago."

Principle 5: Emotions

How do we get people to care about our ideas? We make them *feel* something. In the case of movie popcorn, we make them feel disgusted by its unhealthiness. The statistic "37 grams" doesn't elicit any emotions. Research shows that people are more likely to make a charitable gift to a single needy individual than to an entire impoverished region. We are wired to feel things for people, not for abstractions. Sometimes the hard part is finding the right emotion to harness. For instance, it's difficult to get teenagers to quit smoking by instilling in them a fear of the consequences, but it's easier to get them to quit by tapping in to their resentment of the duplicity of Big Tobacco.

Principle 6: Stories

How do we get people to act on our ideas? We tell stories. Firefighters naturally swap stories after every fire, and by doing so, they multiply their experience; after years of hearing stories, they have a richer, more complete mental catalog of critical situations they might confront during a fire and the appropriate responses to those situations. Research shows that mentally rehearsing a situation helps us perform better when we encounter that situation in the physical environment. Similarly, hearing stories acts as a kind of mental flight simulator, preparing us to respond more quickly and effectively.

(Website: *Made to Stick*)

Availability through
Made to Stick Principles Worksheet

PRINCIPLE	POSSIBLE APPLICATION
Simplicity	
Unexpectedness	
Concreteness	
Credibility	
Emotions	
Stories	

26 Lost in a Big Box World

Story   Chipotle has found much success by offering one dining option: a burrito. Trader Joe's packs its store by offering only one or two kinds of barbeque sauce, not 18 types. Barry Schwartz's *Paradox of Choice* addresses the downsides, and there are many, of too many choices.

A person was once going to buy a productivity-enhancing product from an Internet sales company. He then received three more emails in the course of a week about other options and "better" products. He never did buy anything from them.

Concept   Too much choice limits happiness, creates anxiety, and produces choice paralysis. Limiting consumer choice is often the best policy.

Goal   The goal of this exercise is for participants to understand the concept of the paradox of choice and to use those principles to guide decision making in their organization.

Time   60 minutes

Materials   Choice Audit Worksheet, pens, and corporate communications pieces

Procedure
1. Before the session, assemble your organization's corporate communications pieces.

2. Assemble a group of 5–10 people who are familiar with your organization.

3. Explain the theory of too much choice. You can show the group Schwartz's Ted Talks on the *Paradox of Choice* (18 minutes).

4. Have participants evaluate your organization's offering by referring to its corporate communications pieces in the context of too much or too little choice. Have them use the Choice Audit Worksheet if that is helpful.

Debrief   Some questions that might create interesting discussions include:
1. Are your customers/clients/employees overwhelmed by choice? If so, where?

2. What would be some possible action steps to work with this issue?

3. Is there a longer audit possible where marketing research or a survey would be helpful?

4. Would other employees benefit by being brought into this conversation and/or shown the *Paradox of Choice* Ted Talks?

Personal Application   When and where are you personally overwhelmed and hurt by too many choices? When do you overwhelm loved ones by too many choices?

Choice Audit Worksheet

OFFERING	NUMBER AND TYPE OF CHOICES
Service Offerings	
Product Offerings	
Benefit Offerings	
Other:	
Other:	
Other:	

27 | Which story are you going to tell?

Story
Thirty years ago, a boy was in fifth grade, and his history book told stories of heroes like George Custer, Christopher Columbus, and other white men who conquered and killed other people. Now, the books are telling different stories even though they are using the same facts.

Concept
Any two people can take the same set of facts and make very different stories from them. The concept of "narrative fallacy" is that some of the stories that we create from available facts are not useful and sometimes downright incorrect.

Goal
The goal of this exercise is to recast disempowering stories in your organization.

Time
60 minutes

Materials
Narrative Fallacy Worksheet, paper, and pens

Procedure
1. Assemble a diverse team of 6–8 employees from your organization.

2. Using the Narrative Fallacy Worksheet, have participants brainstorm some of the central stories from your organization. For example, one story might be how the founder slaved away with few resources in a garage for years before successfully marketing the organization's first product. Alternatively, another story might be that no matter what the organization does, the government thwarts its strategies to be successful. Another story might read how the marketing department and the sales department have always been at each other's throats and how it will always be that way.

3. For each story, participants should attempt to construct an alternative story that is just as real, but may be more positive.

Debrief
Some questions that might create interesting discussions include:

1. What are some of the stories you hear around this organization or other organizations?

2. Are any of these "helpless" or "victim" stories? With helpless stories, participants have no power to do anything to help their situations. With victim stories, participants are victims of other people or organizations or regulations. Because they cast themselves as victims, they feel they don't need to do anything to improve their situations.

3. In this organization, are the founders' stories "the only" truth or are they myth, or are they a combination?

4. How can the participants of this exercise help other employees change their stories and therefore become more engaged or empowered to take action and change things for the better?

Personal Application
How do you put together the pieces of your own life? Have you lived a blessed life, or a sad and tragic one?

Narrative Fallacy Worksheet

CURRENT STORY	ALTERNATIVE STORY

28 What is your Black Swan?

Story

Nicolaus Taleb, in his book *Black Swan*, tells the story of 17th century scientists who believed that all swans were white. Then, in the mid-1850s, black swans were observed in Australia and the scientific "facts" had to be changed. Black swans did exist.

Taleb, in this book, shows how "what we do not know" is often more important than "what we know" and yet we focus our time on those things we do know. He suggests that we spend more time discussing the unknowns.

Concept

What we do not know is often more important than what we know. What we do not know can hurt us much more than what we know. Therefore, we should spend more organizational time focused on what we do not know.

Goal

The goal of this exercise is to push participants to spend more time discussing what they do not know and assessing the possibilities of these "unknowns."

Time

45–60 minutes

Materials

Knowns and Unknowns Worksheet and pens

Procedure

1. Assemble a group of 5–10 individuals who are involved in marketing, supply chain management, strategic planning, or a similar discipline.

2. Using the Knowns and Unknowns Worksheet, have the group examine current issues facing your organization. These issues may include competition, industry trends, future product offerings, pricing issues, staffing competencies, etc.

Debrief

Some questions that might create interesting discussions include:

1. What are some of the chief unknowns facing your organization?

2. What are some of the potential downsides of these unknowns?

3. What might be some action plans to minimize these unknowns?

4. How can this group broaden this discussion to include more people in this organization?

Personal Application

How do you weigh the knowns and unknowns in your own life? How can you minimize the downsides of the unknowns?

Knowns and Unknowns Worksheet

ISSUE	KNOWNS	UNKNOWNS

Unit 3:
Group Decision Making

29 Five Fingers to Consensus

Story   A leader approaches his team with an important decision. It is imperative that each team member fully supports the decision. The leader shares the decision with the team and asks for their agreement. Four of the eight team members voice their agreement, and the other four remain silent. The team leader drives toward closure and false consensus without mining the perspective of all team members.

Concept   Team leaders attempt to make consensus decisions in groups all the time. Often they will ask for consensus on a particular decision and take a few positive head nods from select team members as collective agreement. This particular approach can be problematic. If team members do not feel they have a voice in the decision-making process, they are more likely to undermine the decision.

Goal   The goal of this exercise is to recognize the consequences of false consensus and apply the five-finger technique to engage all team members in the consensus decision-making process.

Time   30 minutes

Materials   PowerPoint Slide 29.1 or flipchart and markers

Procedure   1. Display Slide 29.1 or write the following on a flipchart page:

   One Finger: "This is not a good decision and I will work to block it."

   Two Fingers: "I do not agree, but I promise not to get in the way of implementing it."

   Three Fingers: "I do not like it, but I will support it."

   Four Fingers: "It is a good idea and I fully support it."

   Five Fingers: "It is a great idea and I am willing to lead it if necessary."

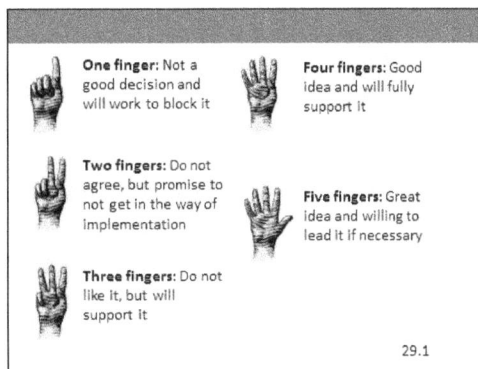

One finger: Not a good decision and will work to block it

Two fingers: Do not agree, but promise to not get in the way of implementation

Three fingers: Do not like it, but will support it

Four fingers: Good idea and will fully support it

Five fingers: Great idea and willing to lead it if necessary

29.1

2. Explain to participants that they can use the five-finger method to explore collective agreement in a group setting.

Exercise 29 (concluded)

3. Share a decision (e.g., "Should we work on case studies in teams for the rest of the workshop?" or "How do you feel about including field trips to small businesses as part of our learning process?") with participants and ask for their perspective using the Five Finger framework.

4. Ask participants to display one, two, three, four, or five fingers depending on their preference.

5. As a facilitator, you should seek individuals who have one, two, or three fingers presented and ask them to share their perspective. Moreover, you should ask them what the leader and/or team can do to persuade them to get on board with the decision of the majority.

Debrief

Some questions that might create interesting discussions include:

1. Can you visualize yourself as a team leader using this method to reach consensus?

2. What are the risks and challenges using a method like this to reach consensus?

3. What should you do if very few people are on board with your proposed decision?

4. Will this approach work every time? Why or why not?

Personal Application

Do you have trouble getting your family and friends to support your proposed decisions? Do others seem to sabotage decisions when you assumed that everyone was in agreement?

30 Divergent AND Convergent...
Best of Both Worlds

Story   A team leader needs the collective wisdom of their team to generate ideas for moving into an emerging market with their new product. Moreover, they need to take the team's ideas and work with them to prioritize the ideas based on the team's preferences.

Concept   When attempting to solve organization issues or capitalize on opportunities, team leaders can increase the effectiveness of their decisions by involving diverse stakeholders in an idea generation process. Moreover, they need to take all potential ideas and narrow several potential ideas down to a manageable number of the most preferred.

Goal   The goal is to use the collective wisdom of the group to identify several ideas for a given topic and then narrow those ideas down to the most preferred by the group.

Time   60 minutes

Materials   Flipchart, markers, colored round sticky dots

Procedure   1. Share the following case study and ask participants to work in groups of 3–5 for 15 minutes and identify a minimum of eight ideas. Ask them to be specific when articulating their ideas. Moreover, ask them to write clearly, capture their ideas on a flipchart, and select a spokesperson who will report out to the large group.

   A Minneapolis store that specializes in wedding dresses has been suffering a significant decline in sales during the past year. Management is unsure about the cause(s) of this loss except that it may be attributed to more aggressive marketing by its competitors (large numbers of direct-mail advertisements, more ad space in local newspapers, more costly window displays, etc.). Because the store is unable to find additional funds for marketing, its management has decided to find new ways to increase the store's marketing and sales efforts without spending more money.

   You have been brought in as a consultant team to work with the marketing to assist in increasing the store's sales?

2. After 15 minutes, ask the spokesperson from each group to post their flipchart page(s) on the wall and share their ideas.

3. Work with the large group to combine ideas or cross out duplicate ideas after all small groups present their ideas.

4. Distribute five colored sticky dots to each participant.

5. Ask each participant to place their sticky dots on the ideas that most accurately reflect their preferences. Explain to participants that they can put all five dots on one idea or they can distribute their dots among choices on any desired choice, e.g., two dots on one idea and three dots on another.

Exercise 30 (concluded)

6. When participants are finished, the ideas with the most colored dots are the most preferred by the group. If there are 20 to 30 ideas, three to five ideas tend to emerge as the most preferred by the group.

7. Work with the group to confirm the top three to five ideas. Once these ideas are confirmed, ask each group to take one idea and develop specific goals and action plans for making the idea a reality.

Debrief

Some questions that might create interesting discussions include:

1. How might you use this process at work?

2. Can you think of variations to the process? If so, explain.

3. How would you narrow the top three choices to one best choice?

Personal Application

How might you use the divergent and convergence process at home? What challenges might you encounter? Will people be patient, creative, and focused when working through the process?

31 ▌The Robbery—The Power of Consensus

Story   A leader is faced with a challenging decision that will have broad implications across the team and organization. They are not sure whether they should involve others in the decision. The leader believes that getting people involved will delay the decision. However, they are hesitant to make a decision because they need the ownership and commitment of the team. Moreover, they need to make the best possible decision because a poor decision could be very costly for the organization.

Concept   When leaders strive for consensus-based decisions, they have the potential of benefiting from the collective wisdom of the decision team. Is there power in numbers when it comes to making decisions collectively? The answer is…it depends. However, if leaders leverage the power of others when making decisions, they will usually make a superior decision. To that end, leaders need to be sure the investment of time is worth the benefits of collective decision.

Involvement is a key leadership practice to ensure you have commitment and ownership, and you have made the right decisions before moving forward with precious organization resources. The trick is knowing who to involve, when, how much, how often, etc. Remember that each situation is different, but before leaders move forward with important decisions, they need to be sure they have laid a foundation for success.

Goal   The goal of this exercise is to demonstrate that team-based (consensus) decision making can yield a better decision than a decision made by one stakeholder.

Time   30 minutes

Materials Robbery Exercise Worksheet, flipchart or whiteboard, markers

Procedure 1. Ask participants to explain the advantages and disadvantages of individual versus team-based (consensus decisions), i.e., individual decision making is faster and consensus decision making is more time consuming.

2. Explain to participants that you would like to test the theory that consensus decisions can be better than individual decisions.

3. Distribute the Robbery Worksheet and tell participants that they have 10 minutes to work individually to answer all of the questions. Be sure to tell them that they have three choices…True, False, or I am not sure (?).

4. After participants complete the worksheet, assemble them into groups of 4 to 5. Ask them to work through the exercise together for 10 minutes and come to consensus. Explain that consensus is not 100% agreement. Moreover, consensus is not the most preferred by every member of the group. A consensus decision is one that all team members can support.

Exercise 31 (continued)

5. After each team completes the exercise, walk through the worksheet and ask teams to share their responses. Most teams will get most of the answers correct.

   Answers: All of the responses except for number 6 are "?". Number 6 is True.

6. Work with the group to scribe all individual scores and team scores on a whiteboard or flipchart. You should notice that most if not all of the individuals do better as a team. Moreover, explain that the individual and team both had the same investment of time…10 minutes.

Debrief

Some questions that might create interesting discussions include:

1. Why do groups tend to make better decisions than individuals?

2. In what instances might an individual make better decisions than a group?

3. What things can you do to maximize the effectiveness of group decisions?

4. What was your strategy for choosing? How effective was it?

5. Were you rushed? If so, how did that impact your results?

Personal Application

Do you make too many important decisions without consulting others? How can you involve others in your important decisions? How can you increase involvement without unnecessarily delaying your decisions?

Robbery Exercise Worksheet

A businessman had just turned off the lights in the store when a man appeared and demanded money. The owner opened a cash register. The contents of the cash register were scooped up and the man sped away. A member of the police force was notified promptly.

For each statement below, circle "T" if you think the statement is True, "F" if you think the statement is False, and "?" if you are not sure.

1.	A man appeared after the owner had turned off his store lights.	T	F	?
2.	The robber was a man.	T	F	?
3.	The man who appeared did not demand money.	T	F	?
4.	The man who opened the cash register was the owner.	T	F	?
5.	The store owner scooped up the contents of the cash register and ran away.	T	F	?
6.	Someone opened a cash register.	T	F	?
7.	After the man who demanded the money scooped up the contents of the cash register, he ran away.	T	F	?
8.	While the cash register contained money, the story does not state how much.	T	F	?
9.	The robber demanded money of the owner.	T	F	?
10.	The story concerns a series of events in which only three people are referred to: the owner of the store, a man who demanded money, and a member of the police force.	T	F	?
11.	The following events in the story are true: someone demanded money, a cash register was opened, its contents were scooped up, and a man dashed out of the store.	T	F	?

32 | Concept Fan

Story Leaders are time compressed and often go with their first impulse when attempting to solve problems. In some cases, this is a very efficient and cost-effective way to make decisions. On the other hand, leaders often find that their first impulse is not always the best solution, especially when stakes are high and the decision is complex with many impacted stakeholders.

Concept Edward de Bono developed the "concept fan" to help decision makers take a step back and look at the whole before making decisions. The concept helps decision makers see several possibilities before making a decision.

Goal The goal of this exercise is to help decision makers see all the possible solutions to a problem before making decisions.

Time 45 minutes

Materials Paper and pens

Procedure
1. Have participants brainstorm a list of community issues; or, if they are part of an intact work group, ask them to brainstorm a list of workplace issues.
2. Assemble participants into small groups of 3 to 5.
3. Ask each small group to select an issue from the list and build a concept fan like the exhibit on the following page that was taken from Toolkitforthinking. com.
4. Ask groups to explain their concept fan to the large group.
5. Ask groups to react to the following questions:
   - Was it difficult building the map? If so, what parts were challenging?
   - Do you believe the process expanded the potential solutions beyond a typical unstructured group discussion?

Debrief Some questions that might create interesting discussions include:
1. In what situations do you need to step back and look at the whole?
2. How might you engage others in helping you develop a concept fan?
3. What are a few possible next steps after you create a concept fan?

Personal Application If you make quick personal decisions and later find yourself saying, "I wish I would have thought of that before moving in this direction?" a concept fan may be a good tool for future decision making. This about important decisions you need to make in the future, sketch some concept fans. Moreover, reflect on how they might influence your decision making.

Reduce pollution from ships

Free oil and rubbish dumps at ports

Monitoring

Improve general water quality

Improve sewage treatment

Block discharge of solids

Control pollution entering the sea

Clean up sea water at local beach

Extend sewage outfalls

Filter sea water

Litter patrols on beach

Contain rubbish dumped at sea

Or eliminate?

Extent to which this returns to beaches?

Control industrial & agricultural pollution

River water monitoring

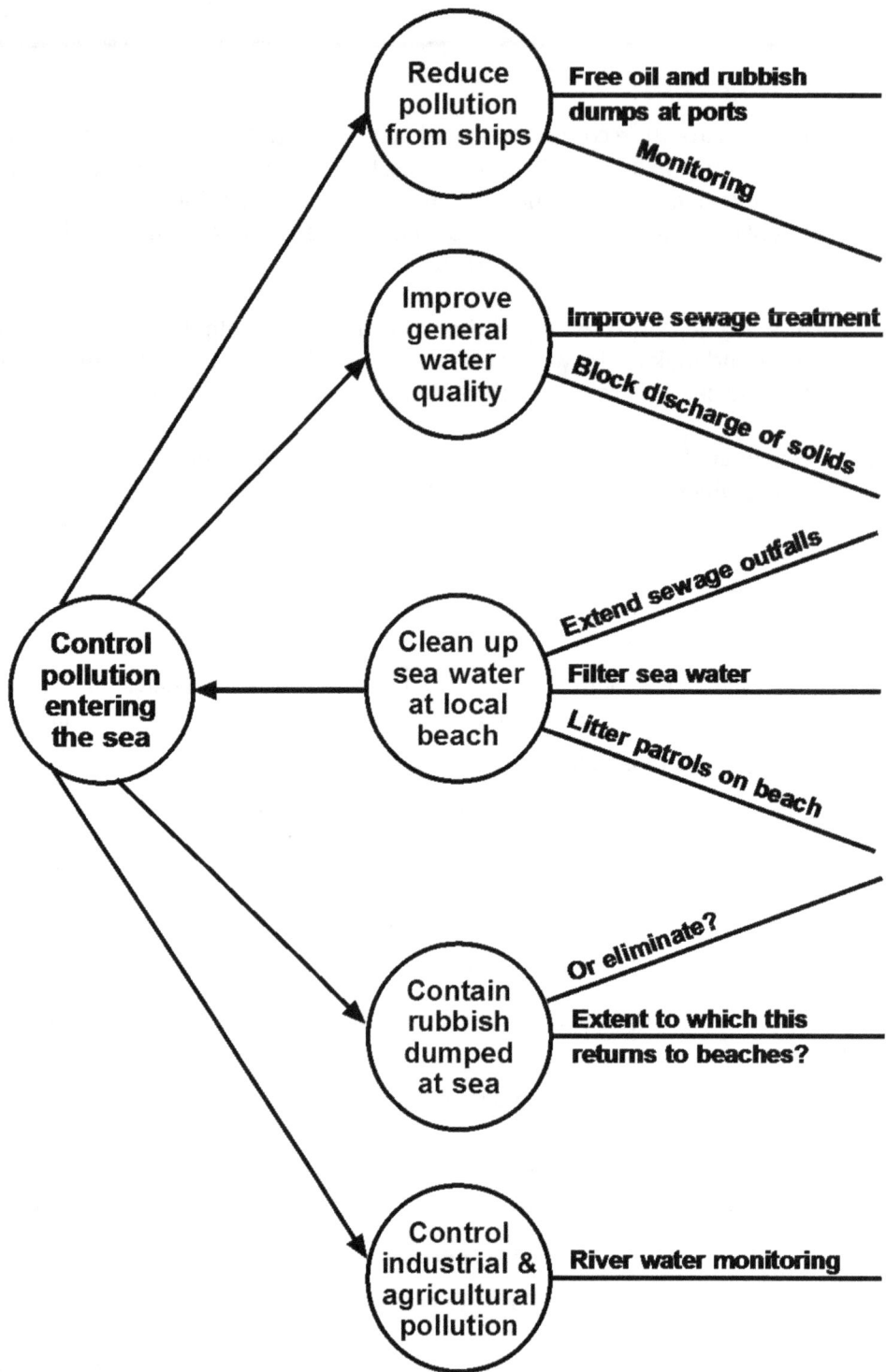

Generating Ideas from a Broader Definition of the Problem

33 | Implications Exploration

Story   Carl makes impulse decisions all the time without thinking through all the implications. He made a quick decision to change the work schedule for his team from five 8-hour days per week to four 10-hour days per week. Carl later experienced turnover in his team, and the organization's customer service satisfaction scores dropped significantly after the decision and subsequent change. Could this have been avoided if Carl had a process to identify implications before making a decision?

Concept   Joel Barker has an excellent online application for building an implications wheel. He suggests that the wheel is used to help people scout the future before making decisions. People make quick decisions all the time without thinking through all the implications. They later find themselves unwinding a poor decision or addressing any number of unintended consequences. Interconnections are a natural part of all complex systems. The key is to understand as many as possible before making a decision.

Goal   The goal of this exercise is to work with multiple stakeholders to identify first-, second-, and third-order implications of decisions.

Time   45 minutes

Materials   Paper and pens

Procedure

1. Explain the concept of decisions and subsequent implications.

2. Assemble small groups of 3–5 participants. Ask them to select a proposed change at work or in the community; e.g., build a new sports stadium, develop a light rail system to connect two cities, move the paint booth from one manufacturing facility to another.

3. Ask participants to identify

   - a proposed change (decision) and place it in a circle in the middle of a blank sheet of paper.

   - five implications of the proposed change, or first-order implications. Have them draw a circle for each around the middle circle and place one implication in each of the circles, then connect each of the five circles to the middle circle with a single line.

   - three implications for each of the five first-order implications, or second-order implications. Have them draw a circle for each and connect them with the first order circles using two lines. See the example on the following page.

4. Explain to participants that they can take the model further and identify third-order implications of second-order implications by linking additional circles to the second-order implications and connecting them with three lines.

Exercise 33 (concluded)

Proposed Change: Build a new football stadium.

First-Order Implication: Restaurant revenues decline during construction.

Second-Order Implication: Tax revenues from restaurants decline.

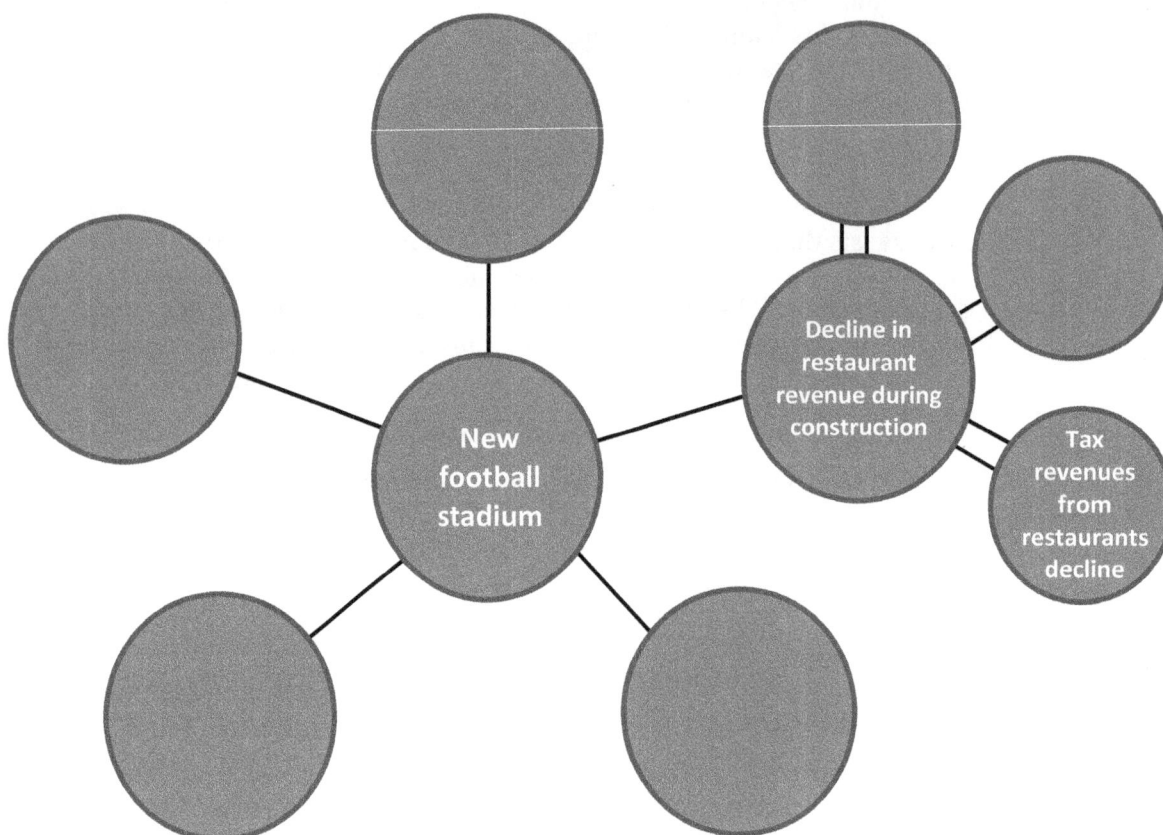

New football stadium

Decline in restaurant revenue during construction

Tax revenues from restaurants decline

*See Joel Barker's **Implications Wheel** at implicationswheel.com

Debrief

Some questions that might create interesting discussions include:

1. How can you use this model to help your team explore implications?

2. What barriers might you encounter?

3. How can you be sure that you do not overwhelm your team with data?

Personal Application

How can you use this concept in your personal life? Can you develop an implication wheel with your family? How can you practice this type of thinking on a daily basis? How can you make this type of thinking automatic?

34 Planning Fallacy

Story
A professor reviewed several hundred student business plans. Most of them overestimated first-year revenues and underestimated first-year expenses. Why? They looked at their business through rose-colored glasses: "Everything will go right."

Concept
The planning fallacy is simply that we build a plan based on everything going right. Seldom does everything go right and so these plans often are not accurate.

Goal
The goal of this exercise is to help participants understand the dynamics of planning and particularly the difficulties of planning for the unexpected.

Time
60 minutes

Materials
Pre-Mortem Planning Worksheet and pens; flipchart and markers

Procedure
1. Assemble a work group of 5 to 15 people who are about to work on a significant project.

2. Discuss the concept of pre-mortem and post-mortem with the group.
   - **Pre-Mortem:** Analyzing beforehand what might go wrong in a situation.
   - **Post-Mortem:** Analyzing after an event what has not gone correctly.

3. Introduce the steps of a pre-mortem exercise (Gary Klein, *The Power of Intuition*):
   - Prepare
   - Imagine a fiasco
   - Generate reasons for failure
   - Consolidate the lists
   - Revisit the plans
   - Periodically review the lists

4. Distribute the Pre-Mortem Planning Worksheet and let the group work through the steps for their project.

Debrief
Some questions that might create interesting discussions include:
1. Have you or anyone you know developed an elaborate plan that went awry? How so?

2. Have you ever participated in a kitchen or other remodeling project? Were there cost overruns or time delays, and why did these happen? Have you ever been involved in wedding planning where there were cost overruns?

3. How can you avoid these awry plans in the future?

4. Are there other tools available?

Personal Application
Where can you put these principles to use for personal plans: Vacation planning? Remodeling? Retirement planning?

Pre-Mortem Planning Worksheet

(Klein, *The Power of Intuition*)

STEP	PROJECT 1	PROJECT 2	PROJECT 3
Prepare			
Imagine a Fiasco			
Generate Reasons for Failure			
Consolidate the Lists			
Revisit the Plan			
Periodically Review the Lists			

Unit 4:
Dysfunctional
Decision Making

35 | The Abilene Paradox

Story   People often decide to do things contrary to the wishes of all members of the team. For example, couples decide to get married when both people have lingering questions about their future together. Teams meet week after week when no one including the leader believes the time is well spent. Why do people and teams make decisions that everyone believes are bad?

Concept   The term *Abilene Paradox* was first introduced by Jerry Harvey. Jerry tells a quirky story about a family that travels from Coleman, Texas, to Abilene when no one in the family wants to go. The famous story ends in conflict and utter confusion. The point is that some teams have trouble managing disagreement. Teams sometimes decide on a course of action that is contrary to the preferences of most or all of their members.

Goal   The goal of this exercise is to help teams recognize the cues and clues that lead to false agreement.

Time   15 minutes

Materials   PowerPoint Slide 35.1, paper, and pens

Procedure   1. Show Slide 35.1 and explain the Abilene Paradox. Provide a few examples: e.g., marriage, team meetings, failed product introductions, the Coleman to Abilene story.

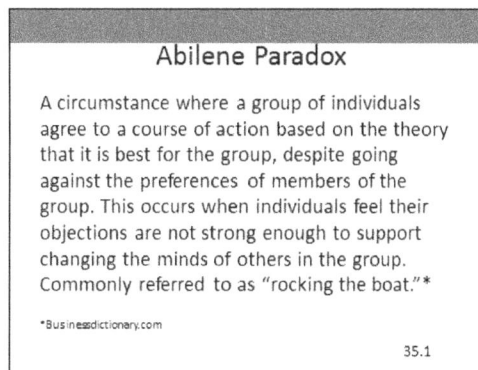

Abilene Paradox

A circumstance where a group of individuals agree to a course of action based on the theory that it is best for the group, despite going against the preferences of members of the group. This occurs when individuals feel their objections are not strong enough to support changing the minds of others in the group. Commonly referred to as "rocking the boat."*

*Businessdictionary.com

35.1

---

2. Ask each participant to work individually for five minutes and identify one personal or professional example. They should use the framework below to articulate their experience:

   - Tell the story: in one paragraph, explain the paradox. Be sure to highlight the outcome.
   - Identify the team members and share their individual perspectives on the decision.
   - Explain why the team failed to manage disagreement.
   - Articulate what any team member could have done to avoid the paradox.

3. Ask at least two members from the workshop to share their experiences.

Exercise 35 (concluded)

Debrief

Some questions that might create interesting discussions include:

1. What are some of the most common signs when a team is on the road to Abilene?

2. What role does the leader play in driving the team to Abilene?

3. What actions do team members take that may suppress the preferences of others?

4. What actions can individual team members do when they suspect that they are on the road to Abilene?

Personal Application

What can you do to be sure your family and friends don't go on the road to Abilene? What things do you do that might influence people to suppress their preferences?

36 The Illusion of Invulnerability

Story   Sally, a vice president, is an optimist; most salespeople are. She has a tendency to foster this optimism in her team as well. When the topic of competition arises and someone tries to elevate warning signs about competitive pressure, Sally is the first to say, "Our competitors will never be able to deliver the quality of products and services that we provide." When Sally does this, the team usually agrees with her and the topic changes. Recently, the organization lost 20% market share to an aggressive competitor. What happened? Could Sally's comments have had something to do with the recent events?

Concept   Irving Janis has coined the term *Groupthink.* Groupthink is team phenomenon that occurs when a teams' excessive drive toward conformity and harmony blind them to effective decision making. One particular symptom of the Groupthink dynamic is The Illusion of Invulnerability. This close-minded approach can limit the critical analysis of the teams' environment, which can lead to faulty decisions.

Goal   The goal of this exercise is to help teams recognize when they are manifesting the "illusion of invulnerability" and how that might impact their decision-making.

Time   20 minutes

Materials   Flipchart or whiteboard, markers, paper, and pens

Procedure   1.   Explain to participants the groupthink phenomenon and more specifically the symptom called illusion of invulnerability where the group is over-confident in its decision-making ability. You can use a family, professional, or political example. A good political example is the bombing of Pearl Harbor: the U.S. military was warned of the potential for attack on the harbor but disregarded it out of a sense of invulnerability.

2.   Ask participants to share some examples and list them on a flipchart. If they are an intact work group, ask them to share specific examples in their organization.

3.   Share several examples to get them started.
   - Bay of Pigs fiasco
   - Vietnam escalation
   - Pearl Harbor
   - Underestimating corporate competition

4.   Assemble participants into groups of 3 to 5 and ask them to select one example. Ask the groups to

   - share their example;

   - identify at least three cues or clues the team could have acknowledged proactively to avoid the illusion;

   - articulate two specific things the leader or the team could have done to avoid the illusion.

Exercise 36 (concluded)

5. Ask each group to select a sponsor from the group to share their example, cues/clues, and potential actions.

6. Summarize the activity by highlighting some key practices for avoiding the phenomenon:

   - Assign a critical evaluator.
   - Remove the leader from select meetings.
   - Bring in an outside expert on the topic.
   - Assign a devil's advocate.
   - Ask the leader to withhold his or her opinion until everyone has spoken.

Debrief

Some questions that might create interesting discussions include:

1. How common is it for teams to slip into the illusion of invulnerability?

2. What role does that leader play in creating the illusion?

3. How can team members help leaders recognize when they are influential in team decision making?

4. Why might this happen to some groups more than others?

5. How willing are you to challenge the prevailing opinion in your work teams?

Personal Application

What role have you played in fostering the illusion? How willing are you to challenge the prevailing opinion of your family and friends when you sense this phenomenon?

37 Decision Fatigue

Story
Researchers studied the decisions of judges in Israel several years ago. Parole was more likely granted in cases listened to in the morning than those pleaded in the afternoon. Why? Judges were fatigued by the afternoon and were more likely to choose the status quo, or "no parole."

Concept
Decision fatigue plagues many of us when we have made many decisions and are called on to make more decisions. Our brains can be too tired to process the necessary information in order to make a coherent, intelligent decision.

Goal
The goal of this exercise is to have participants understand where decision fatigue might impair their decision-making abilities. This process could also be helpful for you and your significant other.

Time
30–60 minutes

Materials
Paper and pens or flipchart and markers

Procedure
1. Assemble your work group.

2. Have participants:

   - write down all the decisions they have made collectively and reach a consensus as to which of these were optimal decisions and which were suboptimal. Ask "Is there any pattern of what caused the poor decisions?"

   - brainstorm and write down all the decisions they make as a group—it could be over the span of a week, month, or year.

   - decide which decisions can be made spontaneously or with little thought (System #1) and those that require more thoughtfulness and reflective thinking (System #2).

   - make a tentative agreement about which decisions the group will make when they are fresh, refreshed, and totally alert and reflective. Ask, "Which decisions can you make quickly, without much reflection?"

3. Discuss if there is a correlation between System #2 decisions and those decisions you *should not* make when you are individually (or collectively) tired.

Exercise 37 (concluded)

Debrief   Some questions that might create interesting discussions include:

1. When have you suffered from decision fatigue? Examples may be during home remodeling, wedding planning, or grocery shopping with children when tired.

2. When have you observed others make poor decisions when they are fatigued?

3. Which decisions or groups of decisions need to be put off until fresh conversations can happen?

4. Which decisions are to be strictly avoided when the group is fatigued?

Personal Application   When do you know you are too tired to make decisions? What are your cues that you are not at an optimal brain space to make a big decision.

38 Halos and Horns

Story   College professors give out halos and horns easily and sometimes wrongly. At a university I taught at, a hockey powerhouse, I found that my students who played hockey were not serious students. As a result, I often graded them poorly and assumed that they did not care about their work.

On the other hand, I gave halos to those who did excellent work. Once a student had written a couple of flawless papers, I barely analyzed their following papers because I was assured they were good writers.

Concept   *The Halo Effect*, written by Dr. Philip Rosenzweig, examines the phenomenon of how past successes and failures cloud our current judgment. The halo effect is another "mental shortcut" that allows us to make pre-judgments (often biased) to save ourselves time. Giving out horns is equally a shortcut.

Goal   The goal of this exercise is to examine how the halo/horn effect lives in our organizations and lives.

Time   30–60 minutes

Materials   Flipchart and markers

Procedure
1. Before the session, find an article by Philip Rosenzweig about the halo effect and send it to participants.
2. Assemble a work group of employees.
3. Explain to participants the concept of the halo effect.
4. Have two pieces of flipchart paper available. Label one "Halos" and the other one "Horns."
5. Ask participants when they (as individuals and as groups or departments) have pre-judged people, products, services, or organizations with a halo or with horns. List these on the corresponding flipchart paper.
6. After approximately 20 minutes of brainstorming, examine the lists and ask which of these receiving halos or horns deserve another judgment or chance at a judgment.

Debrief   Some questions that might create interesting discussions include:
1. Where do we, as an organization, give halos?
2. Where do we, as an organization, give horns?
3. What are the organizational downsides to giving halos and horns?
4. How can we avoid doing so in the future?

Personal Application   When have you unjustly given halos or horns to others? How has that hurt them or you?

39 The Memory Game

Story   When my brother or sister and I speak about our childhood, we remember events so differently. One of us will remember one event and the other two will have no recollection. Sometimes we will remember the tone of an outing differently. Other times we have different ideas about who was even present.

Concept   Memory is flawed at best. Every time a memory is retrieved, it is altered. That is why different people remember events differently.

Goal   The goal of this exercise is to show participants how memory is flawed, and thus they should speak more tentatively of memories.

Time   45–60 minutes

Materials   Flipchart and markers; paper and pens

Procedure
1. Assemble a work group of 5 to 10 participants who have worked together in the past.

2. Have them recollect a shared event at least six months in the past. It could be a product launch, a software glitch, an organizational emergency, a reorganization, or a company picnic.

3. Have participants **individually** write down all the details of the event that they remember.

4. Now brainstorm the details. Write on a flipchart a detail as a participant says it. Place a check mark next to it for each participant who wrote it down on their individual list.

Debrief   Some questions that might create interesting discussions include:
1. Which details do you agree on and which do you disagree on?

2. How might these discrepancies affect decision making?

3. Are your individual memories more or less accurate than your combined memories?

4. What might you do with this realization?

Personal Application   What events might you be remembering inaccurately or only partially? How does that impact your relationships?

40 | Illusion of Causality

Story
One day, I found a plastic baggie of marijuana while cleaning my house. I lectured the young man in question for a while about the dangers of drug use. He replied that his grades had gone up when he started smoking weed. I was not convinced. I tried to explain the difference between causation and correlation.

Concept
Correlation does not equal causation. With correlation, two unrelated events move together (weather patterns and poker hands). With causation, one event causes another (corporate earnings and stock prices).

Goal
The goal of this exercise is to help participants understand that correlation does not create causation, and to see how participants might mix up these two concepts.

Time
30–60 minutes

Materials
Causation/Correlation Worksheet; flipchart and markers; paper and pens

Procedure
1. Assemble a group of 5 to 10 participants.

2. Have the group brainstorm causation statements that they hear in everyday life. Examples might include:

   - Step on a crack, break your mother's back.
   - Bud Light's commercials—"It is not crazy if it works."
   - What goes around comes around.
   - Prayer works.
   - Eat blueberries, fish oil, or dark chocolate and prolong your life.
   - More money spent, higher amount of student learning.
   - Work longer hours, get more work done.

3. Have the group brainstorm organization-sanctioned cause-and-effects. Examples might include:

   - Work at home, get less work done.
   - Spend more money on advertising, sales will rise.
   - Pay more, people will work harder.
   - People who spend more time at their desks are better employees.
   - Employee heroics have kept our company running.

4. Using the Causation/Correlation Worksheet, have the group agree on the level of certainty they have in certain organizational events being causation rather than random correlation.

Exercise 40 (continued)

Debrief   Some questions that might create interesting discussions include:

1. What are organizational blind spots for correlation/causation?

2. When do you personally mix up the two concepts?

3. When does society at large mix up the two concepts?

4. When do commercials want you to mix up the two concepts?

5. What might this work group do to raise its consciousness about the differences between correlation and causation?

6. Where else in this organization should this conversation happen? Over which issues?

Personal   When do you mix up correlation and causation? What harm does that create?
Application

Causation/Correlation Worksheet

First, brainstorm correlation-type events and trends in your organization. Then, rate your confidence that there is causation involved, from 10 = you are totally confident of causation, to 0 = you are sure that there is no causation.

EVENTS	LEVEL OF CONFIDENCE 0 – 10

41 The Wrong Tools

Story   The Neanderthal man roamed the earth for centuries, did fairly well, but then died out. The primary problem with the Neanderthals was that they did not learn from their experience. They never evaluated their decisions to see whether the decisions were good or bad. They just kept doing the same old thing. They used the same tools for 250,000 years. We have no evidence that the Neanderthals ever changed their simple stone scrapers, diggers, and pointers.

Concept   Humans become comfortable using the same tools. These tools may not be the right ones, given the change in times and available technology.

Goal   The goal of this exercise is to have participants examine the tools that they use and consciously decide if they are the appropriate ones.

Time   30–60 minutes

Materials   Tools Worksheet and pens

Procedure   1. Assemble a work group of 5 to 10 participants who are interested in examining how they do their work.

2. Open up the conversation with how many of us have used the wrong tools in our lives, whether in re-modeling projects, or fixing things, or jerry-rigging appliances. (There should be laughter during this conversation.)

3. Have participants broaden the conversation to examine work-related tools using the Tools Worksheet.

Debrief   Some questions that might create interesting discussions include:

1. Which of your tools are outdated?

2. Which tools are easy but not very effective?

3. When do you fall into bad habits when using tools?

4. How can you broaden this conversation for a wider discussion in your organization?

Personal Application   What tools are you emotionally attached to? Which effective tools are you ignoring?

Tools Worksheet

TASK	TOOLS CURRENTLY USED	TOOLS THAT COULD BE USED
Employee Evaluation		
Meetings		
Promoting New Products		
Creating New Processes		
Communicating to Employees		
Motivational Tools		
Other:		
Other:		

42 Throwing Away Tools

Story In a large Montana forest fire in 1947, many firefighters died, overrun by the flames. It is believed that they could have outrun the flames if they had thrown out their heavy tools. However, they did not, and the weight of the tools slowed them down. They carried the tools, up the hill, as the flames overcame them and they died.

Concept We often use the wrong tools because we are afraid to throw them out when they are not useful.

Goal The goal of this exercise is self-examination. Specifically, which tools are we holding on too tightly to, to the detriment of our work or our lives?

Time 45–60 minutes

Materials Wrong Tools II Worksheet and pens

Procedure
1. Assemble a work group of 5–10 people who are interested in examining how work is being done.

2. First, have a broad discussion of things we have a hard time letting go of, primarily for emotional reasons. Some of my list would include:
   - An old sweater
   - My regular toothbrush after receiving an electric one
   - My daughter who has grown up
   - Videos
   - A newspaper made of paper

3. Next, using the Wrong Tools II Worksheet, have the group examine tools that the organization (or individuals within the organization) is using that may be harmful.

Debrief Some questions that might create interesting discussions include:
1. What is hard to let go of?

2. What tools are we wed to even if they are no longer useful?

3. What tools is our society having trouble letting go of? (One PR agency spent several years trying to convince seniors to accept social security payments online rather than with checks in the mail.)

4. What keeps us from letting go?

Personal Application Are you not moving forward in your life because you are embracing the wrong tools?

Wrong Tools II Worksheet

TOOL	PREVIOUS USE	HOW IS IT HARMFUL?

Behavioral Economics and Decision Making

43 Sunk Costs

Story
In the late 1960s, many argued that the United States should not pull out of the Vietnam War because of all the money and lives that we had spent in that war. During the Iraq War recently, the same logic was used.

Concept
Sunk-cost thinking is making decisions based on past decisions. It is like driving by looking in the rear-view mirror.

Goal
The goal of this exercise is to encourage participants to examine where they engage in sunk-cost thinking.

Time
45–60 minutes

Materials
Sunk-Cost Worksheet and pens

Procedure
1. Assemble a work group of 5–10 participants from your organization.
2. Explain the concept of sunk costs. Ask for examples from participants. One might be spending more money on a car that is about to die. Another might be holding on to a stock after its price has receded, hoping for it to rise again.
3. Distribute the Sunk-Cost Worksheet.
4. Have participants look at the way your organization engages in sunk-cost thinking and fill out the worksheet. For example, if the organization might have sunk many resources into developing a product or service that is not selling, the consequences might be that there are not sufficient resources for developing other products. Another option might be to pull the plug on this product or service.

Debrief
Some questions that might create interesting discussions include:
1. Are these situations just isolated examples of sunk-cost thinking or is this organization engaged in systematic sunk cost thinking?
2. Where are the most expansive places that this organization is involved in sunk-cost thinking?
3. How can we begin to remedy these sunk-cost thinking issues?

Personal Application
How am I (along with my significant other) engaged in sunk-cost thinking?

Sunk-Cost Worksheet

PREVIOUS CHOICE	CONSEQUENCES	OTHER OPTIONS
Employees		
Products		
Location		
Market Segments		
Work Process		
Software Solution		
Other:		
Other:		

44 Stuck with Locked Horns

Story

In the mountain wilderness, hikers occasionally come upon two sets of antlers, entangled. Two elk males had been fighting it out, for a female or herd dominance, tangled up their antlers, had been unable to untangle them, and starved to death, together, as a result.

Concept

As humans, we become fixated on adversaries, imagined or real, and remain hooked into an adversarial position with them, to our own detriment. By locking into this other person, or group, we lock up our own energy and thus are engaged in self-defeating behavior.

Goal

The goal of this exercise is to raise self-awareness on how we become locked into adversarial postures and hurt ourselves in the process.

Time

30–60 minutes

Materials

Locked Horns Worksheet, pens, and open minds

Procedure

1. Assemble a work group of 5–10 participants.

2. Discuss the concept of self-defeating behavior and of becoming locked in with adversarial postures.

3. Distribute the Locked Horns Worksheet and have the group work (individually or collectively) on examples of this behavior.

Debrief

Some questions that might create interesting discussions include:

1. What are some of your favorite self-defeating behaviors?

2. What are some of your historic examples of being locked into an adversarial role?

3. What are ways that any of us might lose productivity by being stuck in adversarial roles?

4. What are possible ways out of this posture?

Personal Application

Where do you need to let go of an adversarial posture? If you were to die tomorrow, with whom would you wish to make peace?

Locked Horns Worksheet

ADVERSARY (who or what group)	ISSUE (that caused the adversarial relationship)	WAYS THIS IS SELF-DEFEATING (to you or your organization)

45 Stuck at the End of Your Nose

Story   A leader convenes a strategic planning meeting. Two of the participants begin to talk about a dynamics of a large order being shipped. A couple others talk about the glitches in the new software system. It is difficult to herd in the cats. Why? Because it is so much easier to talk about what we are competent in—operational issues. Talking about strategic planning is more difficult because it is speculative and there are so many unknowns.

Concept   It is easier to think and act operational and to put off strategic thinking until tomorrow and tomorrow and tomorrow.

Goal   The goal of this exercise is to help participants build time and space for strategic, long-term thinking.

Time   60 minutes

Materials   Flipchart, pens, and paper

Procedure
1. Assemble a work group of 5–10 participants.

2. Discuss the importance of long-term thinking and how easy it is to dwell on short-term thinking.

3. Have participants make a list of 20 activities that they do in their job during the course of a month.

4. Have them rate these activities using the following scale: 1 = ease of performing, 2 = long-term vs. short-term orientation.

5. Ask, "Is there any correlation between ease and long-term orientation of these tasks?"

6. Using a flipchart, brainstorm methods, times, and places for long-term thinking. These might include pizza lunches, early morning groups at coffee shops, or trend brainstorming in a conference room. Essentially, participants are looking for ways to build long-term thinking into their routine.

Debrief   Some questions that might create interesting discussions include:
1. What keeps us (individually and collectively) from prioritizing strategic thinking?

2. Does strategic thinking have to be relegated to the formal strategic planning process?

3. Are there methods we can employ to think strategically together?

4. What resources are necessary to do more strategic thinking together?

Personal Application   What kind of strategic thinking are you avoiding in your own life? How can you make time for it?

46 Wooden-Headedness

Story   Mary (not her real name) had a great idea. She, her friends, and their children were enjoying a gorgeous summer weekend in the wilds of western Wisconsin. Why not get some inner tubes and float down the local creek? Her friends suggested that the creek was low, the underbrush was thick, and the mosquitoes were nasty. Mary insisted: "We have to do this and have to have fun." They did tube the creek. They had a miserable time. They were tangled up in fallen branches. They were eaten by mosquitoes. The water was stagnant. The adventure was anything but fun.

Concept   The term originally used by historian Barbara Tuchman (1984), *wooden-headedness* refers to an overly positive, optimistic view of one's own product or idea. Wooden-headedness means to fall in love with one's own idea, and then believe everyone else will love it, too. Venture capitalists call this "sucking your own exhaust" or "drinking your own bathwater."

Goal   The goal of this exercise is to have members of an organization examine their own history of wooden-headedness and raise awareness of the traps of wooden-headedness.

Time   60 minutes

Materials   Wooden-Headedness Worksheet, pens, and open minds

Procedure   1.   Assemble one or two groups from your organization.

                 2.   Discuss with the groups about stubbornness and wooden-headedness.

                 3.   Ask participants: "What are organizational pinch points for stubbornness?" This refers to places and times in an organization where employees can easily, methodically, or systemically revert to being stubborn.

                 4.   Using the Wooden-Headedness Worksheet, have participants brainstorm places of wooden-headedness in the organization.

Debrief   Some questions that might create interesting discussions include:

                 1.   When are we wooden-headed in our own lives?

                 2.   What are arenas where we are blinded to our own wooden-headedness?

                 3.   Why is it so easy to see wooden-headedness in others but not in ourselves?

                 4.   What organizational forces push us into wooden-headedness?

Personal Application   Ask your significant other, parent, sibling, or best friend about where they see stubbornness in you.

Wooden-Headedness Worksheet

Where have you been wrong because of being stubborn?	Impetus for stubbornness:	Remedy in the future:

47 Perfect, or Good Enough

Story

A woman spent months painting and repainting her living room attempting to obtain the exact right tint. Meanwhile, other rooms were neglected and the paint was discolored and chipping.

"If you keep perfecting the buggy whip, but no one wants buggies anymore, then you are wasting your time." (Anonymous)

Concept

Some employees, work groups, and organizations attempt to optimize or perfect certain aspects of their work. These are not always the places or situations to demand excellence.

Goal

The goal of this exercise is for work groups to discuss, agree upon, and decide which parts of their work are worth perfecting. Which parts of their work should be optimized and which should be satisficed?

Time

60 minutes

Materials

Flipchart, paper, and pens

Procedure

1. Assemble a work group of 5–10 employees who share a certain amount of work.

2. Have the group collectively create a list of tasks, outcomes, or jobs that the group has to accomplish.

3. Discuss the concepts of optimization and satisficing. Specifically, what does it look like to achieve "perfection"? What are the costs? What does it look like to satisfice, or to accomplish something "good enough"?

4. Have the group members individually place the tasks, outcomes, and jobs listed in step #2 above into one of two columns: "Optimize" or "Satisfice."

5. Post two flipchart pages on the wall and label them "Optimize" and "Satisfice." Have the group collectively discuss which of their work items should be placed in which column. This should be a lively discussion to facilitate.

Debrief

Some questions that might create interesting discussions include:

1. Which items were easily agreed upon?

2. Which items were more difficult? Why?

3. Have these gaps created disagreements in this work group in the past?

4. Where can there be compromise? Where can there not be compromise?

Personal Application

Where do you try to be perfect? Do those times create duress for you or others in your life?

48 Irrational Thinking

Story   When President George Washington was dying, physicians bled him with leeches. The medical industry, at the time, believed that bleeding would pull bad blood out of a sick person and make them well. Washington died any way.

Concept   Companies that rely on outdated practices need to challenge and reverse established assumptions.

Goal   The goal of this exercise is for participants to challenge their company's or industry's assumptions about doing business.

Time   60 minutes

Materials   Assumptions Worksheet and pens

Procedure   1. Assemble a work group of 5–10 participants who want to look deeply at your company and/or industry.

2. Distribute the Assumptions Worksheet.

3. Have the large group brainstorm several of the underlying industry assumptions. For example, before Amazon, the publishing industry believed that a bookstore was necessary to sell books.

4. Challenge the assumptions. What if they are not true? For instance, do we need a "bricks and mortar" store to sell books?

5. What would be the reverse of these assumptions? For instance, an assumption might be that you need a store to sell books. The reversal would be that you do not need a store to sell books.

6. Is there an innovation in the reversals? The innovation, in this case, might be a system or mechanism to sell books without a bookstore.

Debrief   Some questions that might create interesting discussions include:

1. What are the sacred cows in this industry?

2. What are the sacred cows at this organization?

3. How can we tactfully and politically apply critical thinking to the sacred cows at this company/organization?

4. Are any of these reversals ripe for innovations?

Personal Application   What assumptions are you and your family under for spending your vacations (we always go to the lake for summer vacation)? What are your assumptions for where you spend your money for your family? In addition, what are your assumptions for where you don't spend your money?

Assumptions Worksheet

ASSUMPTION	REVERSE ASSUMPTION	INNOVATION POSSIBILITY

49 Expect Error

Story
An employer installed a parking lot gate that could be raised with the proper identification card. During the first day of the installation, the director of maintenance stood by the gate and showed employees the correct way of swiping their cards in order to gain entrance.

Concept
With simple or complicated systems, users can make errors. Organizations need to anticipate errors in order to make sure that they do not happen.

Goal
The goal of this exercise is for participants to do an audit of the systems in their organization that customers or potential customers may come in contact with and brainstorm ways to avoid these errors.

Time
60 minutes

Materials
Flipchart and pens

Procedure
1. Assemble a group of 5–10 participants who understand your customers well.
2. Brainstorm ways that customers have made errors in consuming settings:
   - Not being able to pump gas
   - Not knowing how to use automated thermostats
   - Not knowing how to apply for a license (of any kind)
   - Not being able to pay for parking with an automated payment system
   - Understanding insurance policies
3. Brainstorm ways that your customers can make errors in using or buying your product or service.
4. Brainstorm ways of preventing or mitigating that error. Are there hotspots where many people typically make errors? Are there patterns of usage?

Debrief
Some questions that might create interesting discussions include:
1. Are there patterns of where customers make errors when dealing with you?
2. Are the patterns avoidable in the first place? For instance, do your operations or manufacturing processes push people toward errors?

Personal Application
Do you always trip on the same step that you have not fixed? Is there a place in your house that always gets dirty? Is mud tracked into your house that could be left outside?

50 | Structure Complex Choices

Story   A daughter anticipating college casually suggested to her father that they should shop for a computer. The myriad of choices was daunting. In addition, the father did not want to leave a new computer in a hot car as they drove across the West in August. They then received a letter from an organization sanctioned by her college that sells six possible computer packages. They could pick it up in the basement of the library upon arrival. What a relief! The decision became easy.

Concept   Our goal as providers and business people should be to help our customers and potential customers simplify their choice making. We should help them simplify complex choices.

Goal   The goal of this exercise is to have participants practice simplifying complex choices.

Time   60 minutes

Materials   Flipchart and pens

Procedure
1. Assemble a cross-functional work group with participants who have direct or indirect contact with your customers or clients.
2. Discuss the concept of complex choices. Have participants give examples of complex choices that they have faced in the past.
3. Have participants map out (on flipchart paper) complex choices that your customers must make in buying or using your product or service.
4. Brainstorm ways to simplify each of these choices. Map out alternatives to each step.
5. If participants come across a time- or labor-saving change in process for customers, create an action plan for implementing it.

Debrief   Some questions that might create interesting discussions include:
1. Where are hotspots where customers can be confused or delayed in using or buying your product or service?
2. How can you address these spots?
3. Do you understand your customers' processes well or excellently?

Personal Application   Is your life set up for simplicity? Alternatively, does your lack of processes make life difficult? For instance, do you keep records of your receipts, donations, etc., in an organized fashion or are you scrambling, looking for paperwork during tax time?

51 We Have Always Done It This Way

Story
Why is our staff meeting always at 2:00 p.m. on Tuesday? Why is our supply chain so convoluted? Why do we need six signatures for a $10 purchase? *Because that is the way we have always done it.*

Concept
The status quo bias is the cognitive bias that the same is the best. Inertia pulls us to what has always been. It is a prejudice for past "what is" against the future "what could be."

Goal
The goal of this exercise is to give participants tools to move past the status quo and become unstuck.

Time
60 minutes

Materials
Beyond Status Quo Worksheet and pens

Procedure
1. Assemble a work group that wants to make some organizational changes.

2. Distribute the Beyond Status Quo Worksheet, and explain the types of potential losses:

   - Identity loss (e.g., if before the change I was the expert in a certain type of software and we are no longer using that software, I would lose that "identity" status)

   - Emotional loss (e.g., if someone leaves the department, others might experience grief at that loss)

   - Control loss (e.g., if there is a reorganization and a person is no longer a department head, he/she might experience a loss of control over that department)

   - Position loss (e.g., a person might lose a committee chair position or a director position)

3. Have participants think about and indicate on the worksheet several changes they would like to see enacted, for example:

   - If the change involves a new software package, a person might lose the identity of being the only one to be able to navigate the old software.

   - A new supply chain might change employees' positions in the organization.

   - A widespread reorganization might create major fear of job loss.

4. Have participants brainstorm the various losses people in the organization would endure if the changes would happen.

5. Have participants brainstorm ways to reduce these losses.

Exercise 51 (continued)

Debrief

Some questions that might create interesting discussions include:

1. What are some organizational pain points—those places that will experience discomfort or pain when a change is enacted? Where can discomfort or rough spots be anticipated?

2. How do we work with these potential losses before we propose changes?

3. Who else should be brought into this conversation?

4. Which of these losses are real and which are imagined?

Personal Application

What changes are you fearful of? What personal losses might occur if there are these changes? How might you lessen the impact of these changes?

Beyond Status Quo Worksheet

POTENTIAL LOSS	CHANGE #1	CHANGE #2	CHANGE #3
Identity			
Emotional			
Control			
Position			

Bibliography

Ariely, D. Three questions on behavioral economics. Retrieved May 12, 2012 from http://danariely.com/2010/07/10/three-questions-on-behavioral-economics/.

Ariely, D. (2008). *Predictably irrational: The hidden forces that shape our decisions.* New York: HarperCollins Publishers.

Ariely, D. (2010). *The upside of irrationality: The unexpected benefits of defying logic at work and at home.* New York: HarperCollins Publishers.

Barker, J. Implications Wheel. Retrieved May 1, 2014 from http://www.joelbarker.com/tools/implications-wheel/.

Brafman, O., & Brafman, R. (2008). *Sway: The irresistible pull of irrational behavior.* New York: Doubleday.

Brilhart, John K., and Gloria J. Galanes. (1989). *Effective group decisions.* Dubuque, IA: William C Brown Publishers: 201-203.

Conrad, L. (March 1, 2013). How industry experts are making sense of behavioral economics. Bank Investment Consultant, Retrieved February, 2013, from www.bankinvestmentconsultant.com/bic_issues/2013_2/how-industry-experts-are-making-sense-of-behavioral-economics-2683549-1.html?zkPrintable=1&nopagination=1.

De Bono, E. (1993). *Serious creativity: Using the power of lateral thinking to create new ideas.* New York: HarperCollins.

Dilliard, A. (1974). *A pilgrim at tinker creek.* New York: Harper's Magazine Press.

Freedman, D. (March/April 2013). Time-warping temptations. *Scientific American Mind, 25,* 45-49.

Gilbert, D. (2005). *Stumbling on happiness.* New York: Random House.

Gillon, S. (2000). *That is not what we meant to do.* New York: W. W. Norton.

Gladwell, M. (2005). *Blink.* New York: Little, Brown, and Company.

Goleman, D. (2006). *Social intelligence: The revolutionary new science of human relationships.* New York: Bantam Books.

Gottman, J. and Silver, N. (2000). *Seven principles for making marriage work.* New York: Three Rivers Press.

Groopman, J. (2007). *How doctors think.* New York: Houghton Mifflin Company.

Grunwald, M. (April 2, 2009). How Obama is using the science of change. *Time,* Retrieved January 12, 2013, from www.time.com/time/magazine/article/0,9171,1889153,00.html.

Hammond J. S., Keeney, R.L. & Raiffa, H. (1999). *Smart Choices: A practical guide to making better choices.* Boston, MA: HBS Press.

Harvey, Jerry B. (1996). *The Abilene paradox and other meditations on management.* San Francisco, CA: Jossey-Bass.

Hawes, D. R. Thinking about time, money and happiness. Retrieved October 18, 2012, from http://www.psychologytoday.com/blog/evolved-primate/201008/happy-times-the-relation-between-time-money-and-happiness.

Heath, C., & Heath, D. (2007). *Made to stick.* New York: Random House.

Heath, C., & Heath, D. (2010). *Switch: How to change things when change is bad.* New York: Random House.

Herbert, W. (January/February 2013). Finding self-discipline in others. *Scientific American Mind 23,* 66–67.

Janis, I. (1982). *Groupthink: Psychological studies of policy decisions and fiascoes* (2nd ed.). Boston, MA: Houghton Mifflin.

Johnson, B. Polarity management. Retrieved May 9, 2014 from http://www.polaritypartnerships.com/

Kahane, A. (2007). *Solving tough problems: An open way of talking, listening, and creating new realities.* San Francisco, CA: Berrett-Koehler Publishers, Inc.

Kahneman, D. (2011). *Thinking, fast and slow.* New York: Farrar, Straus and Giroux.

Lambert, C. (March–April 2006). The marketplace of perceptions: behavioral economics explains why we procrastinate, buy, borrow, and grab chocolate on the spur of the moment. *Harvard Magazine,* 50–57 & 93–95.

Loewenstein, G., Brennan, T., & Volpp, K. (November 2007). Asymmetric paternalism to improve health behaviors. *The Journal of the American Medical Association, 298,* 2415–2417.

Miron-Shatz, T. How behavioral economics can make you exercise. Retrieved June 16, 2012, from http://www.psychologytoday.com/blog/baffled-numbers/201110/how-behavioral-economics-can-make-you-exercise.

Nobel, C. (February 13, 2013). 5 Weight loss tips from behavioral economics. HBS Working Knowledge. Retrieved February 19, 2013, from http://hbswk.hbs.edu/item/7210.html.

Saporito, B. (February 4, 2013). Staying power. New ways companies are getting us to stick with lousy service. *Time, 181,* 4, 1.

Schwartz, B. (2004). *The paradox of choice: Why less is more.* New York: HarperCollins Publishers.

Senge, P. (1990). *The fifth discipline: The art and practice of the learning organization.* New York: Currency Doubleday.

Shirky, C. (2010). *Cognitive surplus: Creativity and generosity in a connected age.* New York: Penguin.

Scholtes, Peter R. (1988). *The team handbook how to use teams to improve quality.* Madison, WI: Joiner Associates Inc.

Stewart, S. (February 2005). Can behavioral economics save us from ourselves? *University of Chicago Magazine,* 97, Retrieved November 10, 2012, from http://magazine.uchicago.edu/0502/features/economics.shtml.

Surowiecki, J. (January 21, 2013). That sunk-cost feeling. *The New Yorker,* 24.

Szalavitz, M. (January 1, 2008). 10 Ways we get the odds wrong. *Psychology Today,* Retrieved January 11, 2013, from http://www.psychologytoday.com/articles/200712/10-ways-we-get-the-odds-wrong.

Thayer, R. & Sunstein, C. (2008). *Nudge: Improving decisions about health, wealth, and happiness.* New Haven: Yale University Press.

Van Hecke, M. L. (2007). *Blind spots: Why smart people do dumb things.* New York: Prometheus Books.

Volpp, K. G., Asch, D. A., Galvin, R., & Loewenstein, G. (August 4, 2011). Redesigning employee health incentives—lessons from behavior economics. *The New England Journal of Medicine, 365,* 388–390.

Watkins, M. (2004). *The first 90 days: Critical success strategies for new leaders at all levels.* Boston, MA: Harvard Business School Press.

Welch, N. (February 2010). A marketer's guide to behavioral economics. *McKinsey Quarterly,* Retrieved September 22, 2012, from http://www.mckinseyquarterly.com/A_marketers_guide_to_behavioral_economics_2536.